MAY 2003

A BASIC GUIDE TO

Softball

An Official U.S. Olympic Committee Sports Series

The U.S. Olympic Committee

Griffin Publishing Group

ISBN 1-58000-074-6

10 9 8 7 6 5 4 3 2 1

Printed in the United States of America

Editorial Statement
In the interest of brevity, the Editors have chosen to use the standard English form of address. Please be advised that this usage is not meant to suggest a restriction to, nor an endorsement of, any individual or group of individuals, either by age, gender, or athletic ability. The Editors certainly acknowledge that boys and girls, men and women, of every age and physical condition are actively involved in sports, and we encourage everyone to enjoy the sports of his or her choice.

Griffin Publishing Group
2908 Oregon Court, Suite I-5
Torrance, CA 90503
Tel: (310)381-0485 Fax: (310)381-0499

ACKNOWLEDGMENTS

PUBLISHER	Griffin Publishing Group
DIR. / OPERATIONS	Robin L. Howland
PROJECT MANAGER	Bryan K. Howland
WRITER	Suzanne Ledeboer
BOOK DESIGN	Midnight Media

USOC
CHAIRMAN/PRESIDENT   William J. Hybl

ASA/USA SOFTBALL
PRESIDENT   G. Pat Adkinson
EXECUTIVE DIRECTOR   Ron Radigonda

EDITORS   Geoffrey M. Horn
                       Catherine Gardner
PHOTOS   ASA/USA Softball
                       National Softball Hall of Fame
                       Doug Hoke
                       International Softball Federation
COVER DESIGN   m2design group
COVER PHOTO   USA Softball/Doug Hoke
ATHLETE ON COVER   Lisa Fernandez

Special thanks to Ron Babb of USA Softball for his expertise and extraordinary good will in helping bring this book to completion. Also, grateful acknowledgment is extended to Premier's Sport Awards Program for the use of selected softball technique illustrations.

THE UNITED STATES OLYMPIC COMMITTEE

The U.S. Olympic Committee (USOC) is the custodian of the U.S. Olympic Movement and is dedicated to providing opportunities for American athletes of all ages.

The USOC, a streamlined organization of member organizations, is the moving force for support of sports in the United States that are on the program of the Olympic and/or Pan American Games, or those wishing to be included.

The USOC has been recognized by the International Olympic Committee since 1894 as the sole agency in the United States whose mission involves training, entering, and underwriting the full expenses for the United States teams in the Olympic and Pan American Games. The USOC also supports the bid of U.S. cities to host the winter and summer Olympic Games, or the winter and summer Pan American Games, and after reviewing all the candidates, votes on and may endorse one city per event as the U.S. bid city. The USOC also approves the U.S. trial sites for the Olympic and Pan American Games team selections.

WELCOME TO THE OLYMPIC SPORTS SERIES

We feel this unique series will encourage parents, athletes of all ages, and novices who are thinking about a sport for the first time to get involved with the challenging and rewarding world of Olympic sports.

This series of Olympic sport books covers both summer and winter sports, features Olympic history and basic sports fundamentals, and encourages family involvement. Each book includes information on how to get started in a particular sport, including equipment and clothing; rules of the game; health and fitness; basic first aid; and guidelines for spectators. Of special interest is the information on opportunities for senior citizens, volunteers, and physically challenged athletes. In addition, each book is enhanced by photographs and illustrations and a complete, easy-to-understand glossary.

Because this family-oriented series neither assumes nor requires prior knowledge of a particular sport, it can be enjoyed by all age groups. Regardless of anyone's level of sports knowledge, playing experience, or athletic ability, this official U.S. Olympic Committee Sports Series will encourage understanding and participation in sports and fitness.

The purchase of these books will assist the U.S. Olympic Team. This series supports the Olympic mission and serves importantly to enhance participation in the Olympic and Pan American Games.

United States Olympic Committee

Contents

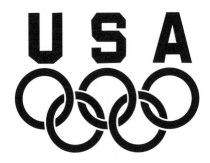

AN ATHLETE'S CREED

The most important thing in the Olympic Games is not to win but to take part, just as the most important thing in life is not the triumph but the struggle. The essential thing is not to have conquered but to have fought well.

These famous words, commonly referred to as the Olympic Creed, were once spoken by Baron Pierre de Coubertin, founder of the modern Olympic Games. Whatever their origins, they aptly describe the theme behind each and every Olympic competition.

Metric Equivalents

Wherever possible, measurements given are those specified by the Olympic rules. Other measurements are given in metric or standard U.S. units, as appropriate. For purposes of comparison, the following rough equivalents may be used.

1 kilometer (km)	= 0.62 mile (mi)	1 mi = 1.61 km
1 meter (m)	= 3.28 feet (ft)	1 ft = 0.305 m
	= 1.09 yards (yd)	1 yd = 0.91 m
1 centimeter (cm)	= 0.39 inch (in)	1 in = 2.54 cm
	= 0.1 hand	1 hand (4 in) = 10.2 cm
1 kilogram (kg)	= 2.2 pounds (lb)	1 lb = 0.45 kg
1 milliliter (ml)	= 0.03 fluid ounce (fl oz)	1 fl oz = 29.573 ml
1 liter	= 0.26 gallons (gal)	1 gal = 3.785 liters

Softball and the Olympics

Softball is a relatively new event at the Olympic Summer Games, having appeared for the first time at Atlanta in 1996. However, hitting round objects with sticks or clubs (later named bats) has a history as a form of recreation that stretches back several centuries.

Early Ball and Stick Games

Balls that were made from leather, then stuffed with feathers and hand–sewn were used by Egyptians, Greeks, and Romans to play catch. Tossing balls was so popular that even the public baths in Rome had separate rooms for the activity, which was not a game, but was, instead, for exercising and conditioning. When balls weren't available, stones were kicked around—probably a very early form of the children's game "kick the can" or rudimentary soccer. Balls made from rubber were in general usage by the Aztec Indians and were noted by fifteenth-century visitors. Jai alai games in Spain used a rubber ball years before other Europeans adopted the new material.

From catching a ball to hitting one with a stick, bat, or club was the next logical development along the way to the ball and bat sports of the nineteenth and twentieth centuries. Ball and stick games are depicted on urns and in friezes (a band of sculpture or decoration around the top of a wall or building), evidence that these early games were played by American Indians, Greeks, and Persians. The latter knew, and perhaps played, a form of polo as early as 522 B.C. The modern game of golf is credited to the Scots, but variants reach back to Roman times.

Space to play catch or bat a ball was always an important consideration, but simple games using just a ball could be played easily in small, enclosed spaces—a courtyard, for example. Larger areas, such as a village green or open field, were needed when ball and bat games became popular outdoor activities for participants and spectators. Especially popular in England were two games—cricket and "rounders," the latter a bat and ball game that baseball historians believe is an offshoot of cricket and the foundation for modern baseball.

As England's empire expanded globally so did the game of cricket, except in her former American colonies. There, rounders, in various forms, was widely popular. Also known as townball, stickball, postball, and even baseball, the game was played usually by two teams of nine men each. Matches were two innings, with each team batting until all nine players were out. The object then, as now, was to score more "rounders" (runs) than the opposition. Baseball developed from this rather unruly and unregulated ball and bat game, and was recognized as the national American pastime by the mid–nineteenth century. The development of softball was not far behind.

The Birth of Softball

Over 100 years ago in Chicago, a group of young men—all Harvard and Yale graduates—waited at the Farragut Boat Club's gymnasium on Thanksgiving Day to learn the results of the annual Yale–Harvard football game. The news that Yale had won (17-8) set off a celebration, with a Yale grad throwing a rolled up boxing glove to a Harvard alum, who then swung at it with a stick. Thus was born indoor baseball, which eventually, because of its big, soft ball, became today's softball. (The final score was 41-40.)

The genius behind this new game was George Hancock, a reporter for the Chicago Board of Trade, who tied up the laces of a boxing glove to create a ball, devised the playing diamond, wrote the rules, and enlisted members from other local gyms as opponents. He did use some rules from baseball, but adapted the playing field to fit inside a gymnasium by shortening the distances between bases and from the pitcher's spot to home plate. No other team sport had been played inside a gymnasium; softball was the first. Once winter ended, the game moved outside, where it was played on small, gymnasium–sized fields.

Hancock, who was the first recognized authority on this new game—after all, he invented it—drew up the list of rules that became official in 1889. Still, the game was known as indoor baseball until the name softball was coined by Walter Hakanson in 1926, but it didn't become softball officially until the next decade.

The sport had several names, depending on locality—kitten ball, recreation ball, mush ball, and diamond ball. Regardless of its name, softball spread rapidly to other areas, notably Minnesota, where a fireman, Lt. Lewis Rober, had his firemen play to keep fit for their strenuous jobs. Shortly after the turn of the century, Minneapolis had a softball league, and by 1906 there was an official rule book.

Softball in 1931. National Softball Hall of Fame

Other softball groups formed, all attempting to establish unified rules and regulations for the game. Committees met and eventually two national softball tournaments were held— the first in 1931 in Minneapolis and the second in 1933 in

Milwaukee. Even with divided organization beyond the local level, softball became more and more popular in the 1920s and 1930s.

A further impetus to its growth was the financial aid and publicity given by newspapers in their sports pages, especially those in the Hearst group. Radio broadcasts of important games added to softball's growing popularity, as did the construction by the Works Progress Administration (WPA) of athletic fields with softball diamonds. This could not have happened at a better time for Americans, who, in 1933, were in the midst of the severest economic depression in U.S. history.

In Chicago, where softball began in 1887, Leo Fischer, sports editor of *The Chicago American,* along with his friend M. J. Pauley, a sporting goods salesman, organized local softball tournaments. These were so popular that Fischer and Pauley decided something larger and more inclusive was needed to promote the game they loved. It was their idea to hold the first national championship tournament at the 1933 Century of Progress Chicago World's Fair.

There was little, if any, money for recreation, but watching softball was free, and the World's Fair drew teams from 16 states for the first national softball championship. Competitors were divided into three divisions: fast pitch, slow pitch, and women, and all three were won by Chicago teams. The crowds attending the Fair loved the game and 70,000 spectators watched the first round of play. When a second national championship was held, it was also in Chicago. This time 30 states sent teams, there were 1,000 players, and 200,000 spectators watched. A local team from Chicago won the women's title, while the men's title went to a team from Wisconsin. Softball had arrived, but it still needed organization.

National Softball Hall of Fame

Southern Regional ASA Women's Tournament
in 1954. R/L: Bonnie Roberts of Oak Ridge, Tennessee;
Frances Wallace of Atlanta Lorlei Ladies

The Amateur Softball Association

Fischer and Pauley learned at the World's Fair national championships that most teams played by their own rules, had no overall governing body, and used different equipment. They decided to rectify this by founding the Amateur Softball Association (ASA) in 1933 and providing softball with a national group that codified the rules under a Joint Rules Committee, directed the growth of the sport, and adopted officially the name softball. Leo Fischer became ASA's first president, and within three years, all member teams played the same game. By the end of the 1930s, the ASA reported that over 6 million people (5 million male and 1 million female) were playing the game.

World War II spread softball to a global following of players and fans in nearly 100 countries, and the game had its own heroes. One was Herb Dudley, who in a 1949 national championship game, had 55 strikeouts in 21 innings of play—the equivalent of three regular-length games.

The Raybestos Brakettes team of Stratford, CT, was founded in 1947 and won 23 national titles. The team was noted for the strong pitching of Joan Joyce, who had 105 no-hitters in over 500 games. (Some of her pitches were clocked at 100 miles per hour.) Joyce led the United States to its first world championship in 1974 with a record-setting performance of: strikeouts (76); earned run average, or ERA (0.00); consecutive scoreless innings (36); most no-hit, no-run games (3); and most perfect games (2).

Four decades later, the Men of Steele, a slow pitch team from Tampa, FL, was known for its home run hitting prowess. One player, Mike Macenko, hit 3,143 home runs over a period of seven years, but his best year was 1987 when he hit 844.

ASA/USA Softball/Ron Babb

Allegiance to the flag. An honor to wear the red, white, and blue.

Unlikely as it may seem, softball is the number-one adult participation sport in Alaska. There are more slow pitch softball teams per capita in our 49th state than all but 4 of the 50 states. Imagine playing in an insulated ski jacket when the temperature is 0 degrees Farenheit, and the wind is blowing at 30 MPH. That's a wind-chill factor of -49° F. Or, imagine playing in snow in July, which is standard in the far northern part of the state. Since 1996, 15 amateur teams from Alaska have qualified for national tournaments, and Michele Granger of Anchorage was a member of the 1996 gold medal team at Atlanta.

Slow pitch softball eventually replaced fast pitch as the popular form of the game because it allowed more players at all skill levels the opportunity to participate. This is reflected in the growth of registered slow pitch teams. By 1994, 90 percent of teams under the auspices of the ASA were slow pitch teams.

The need for an international organization had become obvious and, in 1952, the International Softball Federation (ISF) was formed to organize all national softball associations; to obtain recognition from the International Olympic Committee (IOC); and to have softball included in national and international sporting events, especially the Olympic Summer Games.

A world tour was organized in 1965, and the first Women's Fast Pitch Tournament was held in Melbourne, Australia. Softball was a demonstration event at the Asian Games and the Pan American Games in the 1960s. In 1970, Japan hosted and won the second world championship; the third in 1974 was in Stratford, CT, with the U.S. team gaining the title. The U.S. has an outstanding record in World Championship play and has captured the last four ISF World Championships. U.S. teams have won the last four Pan American Games, the 1999 Canada Cup, and the 1999 U.S. Olympic

Cup. Even with all these gold and silver medals at world championships and Pan American Games, it has taken 20 years for the media to recognize these smart, talented, and dedicated women athletes.

Today, the ASA is the National Governing Body (NGB) for softball in the United States and works with the U.S. Olympic Committee to select and train the players who compete for America in international competitions. The ASA oversees 101 state and metro associations that make up its national organization. These local groups register the teams that play under ASA's programs. There are more than 30 other groups affiliated with the ASA, including International Senior Softball, the Athletic Association for the Deaf, Special Olympics International, and the Armed Forces.

ASA/USA Softball/Ron Babb
**We're No.1! U.S. Softball team, the best in the world
championships, Pan Am Games, Olympics**

Currently, the ASA oversees 260,000 teams with more than 4 million members. There are nearly 40 million amateur softball players in the United States alone, with an estimated 20 million in other countries. The ASA and USA Softball:

- Promote amateur softball for everyone, without discrimination.

- Determine and update all rules and regulations, including ethics and sportsmanship.

- Encourage active participation in the ASA by all amateur softball groups at state, regional, or national levels.

- Conduct amateur softball championships at local, state, regional, and national levels.

- Develop clinics, seminars, and training materials to aid in teaching the skills and rules of softball.

The national headquarters, with a professional staff of 30, is located in Oklahoma City on an 20-acre complex. Expansion plans include a USA Softball National Team Training Facility complete with dorms, food service, sport-specific training equipment, and workout areas. Eventually, athletes will be able to train year-round and receive coaching from top-flight instructors. The complex includes the National Softball Hall of Fame Museum and Hall of Fame Stadium.

The National Softball Hall of Fame Museum, founded in 1957, is a facility that traces the history of softball and is educational as well. Visitors can learn how equipment is made, watch softball videos, and see displays honoring individuals who helped to promote the sport, even though they weren't players. The ASA Research Center and Library answers questions, and contains an extensive collection of publications and videos. It also serves as the official archive for softball.

The Hall of Fame honors players from Women's Slow and Fast Pitch, plus players from Men's Fast Pitch, Modified Pitch, and Slow Pitch. The Hall of Honor recognizes nonplayers—

commissioners, umpires, managers, sponsors, and those who have given meritorious service—for their special contributions to the sport of softball.

The most recent addition to the Hall of Fame Museum is an Olympic Gallery that showcases the long road to Atlanta.

Hall of Fame Stadium has 2,046 permanent seats, with an expanded capacity of nearly 6,000. It is the official training facility of USA Softball and is the home field for the teams that represent the United States in international competitions. Additionally, the stadium is used every year for softball competitions, including the National Collegiate Athletic Association's (NCAA) Women's College World Series, Anyone Can Play Softball Game (physically challenged), Beep Ball Bombers (blind), and the NAACP National Championships.

ASA/USA Softball/Doug Hoke

Softball star Dr. Dot Richardson making a play against China

Atlanta – 1996

The ASA built a women's fast pitch softball team to represent the United States by starting with a tryout program at the local level. There were minimum standards to qualify. For example, pitchers needed a fastball that traveled 55 mph; a change-up of 10 mph slower. Catchers needed a throwing speed of 55 mph and a running speed from home to first base of 2.95 seconds. Infielders and outfielders met a throwing speed of 55 mph. All players had to run a mile in 8.5 minutes, maximum; perform 65 crunches in 60 seconds; and run from home to home in 12.5 seconds. Conditioning mattered.

These tryouts continued through the Pan American Games and the 1995 Olympic Festival until the best women's fast pitch softball players in the United Staes. were winnowed down to 67 finalists; 15 were chosen for Team USA.

They toured coast-to-coast between September 1995 and April 1996, compiling a 60-1 win/loss record. Then, the team settled down to four months of practice in Georgia to prepare for the eight-nation tournament. Team USA finished 8-1, its final win by a score of 3-1 over China's team, giving Team USA the first-ever gold medal in softball at an Olympic Summer Games.

Between Atlanta and Sydney, the USA Softball Team didn't rest on its laurels. It continued to compete on the national and international levels, winning more championships and medals.

Two years after Atlanta, the team won a gold medal at the 1998 South Pacific Classic in New Zealand and followed this victory with its fourth consecutive gold medal at the ISF Women's World Championship in Fujinomiya, Japan. In 1999 the team won gold medals at three different competitions: the Canada Cup, the Pan American Games, and the U.S. Olympic Cup.

By midyear 2000 the team had played 45 games against college and professional teams, winning all of them.

Sydney – 2000

The IOC decided that women's fast pitch softball would be included in the 2000 Games at Sydney, and tryouts for this team began in 1998.

Female U.S. citizens were eligible, and once all applications were reviewed by the Women's National Team Selection Committee, potential team members were invited to participate in the Preliminary Olympic Trials held in September 1998. Minimum requirements are outlined below.

Infielders/Outfielders

Players must meet these five requirements:

- Bat speed of 50 mph minimum
- Throwing speed of 55 mph minimum
- Run from home to first base in 2.95 seconds maximum
- Run from home to home in 12.50 seconds maximum
- Do 30 push-ups

Pitchers

Pitchers must do any three of the following five pitches with consistent speed:

- Fastball   55 mph minimum
- Curveball   55 mph minimum
- Riseball   55 mph minimum
- Dropball   55 mph minimum
- Change-up   45 mph maximum, or 18 mph slower than maximum pitch speed

Catchers

Catchers must meet these six requirements:

- Throw from home to second base in 2.0 seconds maximum

- Bat speed of 50 mph minimum

- Throwing speed of 55 mph minimum

- Run from home to first base in 2.95 seconds maximum

- Run from home to home in 12.50 seconds maximum

- Do 30 push-ups

Softball Biographies

USA Softball Team Roster - 2000 Olympic Summer Games

Player	Position	Ht.	B/T
Christie Ambrosi	Left field	5'8"	L/R
Laura Berg	Center field	5'6"	L/L
Jennifer Brundage	Third base	5'7"	R/R
Crystl Bustos	Shortstop	5'8"	R/R
Sheila Douty	First base	5'10"	R/R
Lisa Fernandez	Pitcher/Third base	5'6"	R/R
Lori Harrigan	Pitcher	6'1"	R/L
D. Henderson	Pitcher	6'1"	R/R
Jennifer McFalls	Ut. Inf.	5'6"	R/R
Stacey Nuveman	Catcher	6'0"	R/R
L. O'Brien-Amico	Right field	5'9"	L/L
Dot Richardson	Second base	5'5"	L/R
Michele Smith	Pitcher	5'10"	L/L
M. Venturella	Catcher	5'10"	L/L
Christa Williams	Pitcher	5'7"	R/R

Alternates

Amanda Freed	Pitcher	5'8"	R/R
Teri Klement-Goldberg	Utility	5'10"	R/R
Amanda Scott	Pitcher	5'9"	R/R
Shelly Stokes	Catcher	5'5"	R/R
Dani Tyler	Ut. Inf.	5'6"	R/R

Christie Ambrosi

Christie, from Overland Park, KS, attended UCLA, where she played for the 1999 NCAA Softball National Champions and was named a first-team National Fastpitch Coaches Association (NFCA) All-American, All-Pacific, and All-PAC 10 member. She was a silver medal-winner at the 1999 Coca-Cola USA Softball Women's National Team Festival.

In international competition, the outfielder was a member of the USA Gold Team that won the Canada Cup in 1999. She had nine hits, six RBIs, and scored five runs when the USA Team won gold at the 1999 Pan American Games. Christie gave the U.S. another fine performance at the Olympic Cup, where she batted .333, had four RBIs, and scored one run.

Laura Berg

Centerfielder Laura Berg, from Santa Fe Springs, CA, is said to "own" the outfield, chasing down what at first appear to be sure hits and turning them into easy outs.

Laura has been on U.S. gold-medal teams since 1994, beginning with the Women's World Championship, then the Superball Classic in 1995, and ending with the Olympic Summer Games in Atlanta, where she made a spectacular catch against the Dutch team.

Laura helped the USA Gold Team with thirteen hits, scored eight runs, and had eight RBIs, with a .371 batting average, at the 1999 Canada Cup. Her batting average of .385 helped the USA Team win gold at the 1999 Pan American Games, where Laura had fifteen hits (three of them doubles), drove in six runs, and scored six. Her batting average stayed above .300 at the 1999 U.S. Olympic Cup, where she and the team were gold-medalists.

An NCAA All–American in 1994 and 1995, Berg plays at Fresno State University, where she compiled a string of ninety–nine consecutive games without an error.

Jennifer Brundage

Jennifer Brundage, an alternate on the 1996 Olympic Team, made the roster for Sydney. The standout at third base played her college ball at UCLA, where she received the 1995 Honda Award as the nation's top collegiate softball player.

Nationally, she was a gold medalist at the 1999 Coca-Cola USA Softball Women's National Team Festival, but her most recent achievements have been on the international level.

Jennifer had a double, a home run, four RBIs, and a .250 batting average when the USA Team won a gold medal in the 1998 South Pacific Classic. With the USA Gold Team at the 1999 Canada Cup, Brundage had a .400 batting average. Her ten hits (including two home runs) netted six runs scored and six RBIs. At the 1999 Pan American Games, she hit .281, drove in three runs, and scored six. Jennifer contributed at the 1999 U.S. Olympic Cup where she started three games and scored one run.

Crystl Bustos

Crystl plays shortstop for the Akron Racers of the Women's Professional Softball League and was named a 1999 WPSL All-Star. During her junior college career at Palm Beach Community College in Lake Worth, FL, Crystl hit .614. She had 135 hits, which included 26 doubles, 14 triples, 23 home runs, and 102 RBIs.

Internationally, Crystl was a member of the USA Gold Team at the 1999 Canada Cup. She hit five home runs, but the biggest and best was a three-run shot that gave the Gold Team a 6-3 victory over Japan. Altogether, Crystl batted .419, had thirteen hits, scored eleven runs, and drove in nine. She upped her average to .439, had eighteen hits, and fifteen RBIs as a member of the gold-medal USA Team at the 1999 Pan American Games. She finished 1999 at the U.S. Olympic Cup with five hits, a .385 batting average, one RBI, and five runs scored.

Sheila Douty

Sheila was a member of the USA Softball National Team that won the gold medal in the 1996 Olympic Games. She led the USA Team to the gold medal at the 1998 South Pacific Classic in Christchurch, New Zealand, and was named "Most Outstanding Hitter" of the tournament after batting a team-best .476 with two doubles, a triple, a home run, and a team-leading nine RBIs. She went on to win a gold medal in the 1998 ISF Women's World Championships at Fujinomiya, Japan; and at the 1999 Canada Cup, where she had a batting average of .346, had nine hits (two of them doubles), scored three runs, and had three RBIs. Sheila continued to help her team win gold medals at the 1999 Pan American Games as she batted .355, had six RBIs, and scored four runs. During the 1999 U.S. Olympic Cup, Sheila hit a two-run homer in the bottom of the seventh inning to give the U.S. a 3-2 victory over Australia.

She was a member of the USA teams that won the silver medal at Superball '97 and the gold medal at Superball '95 (both held in Columbus, GA); the gold medal at the 1995 Pan American Games; and the gold medal at the 1994 ISF Women's World Championships in St. John's, Newfoundland, Canada. On the national level, she was a member of the East squad that captured the gold medal at the 1997 USA Softball National Team Festival in Midland, MI; was a gold-medal winner at the 1994 U.S. Olympic Festival in St. Louis, MO; and has been an eleven-time ASA All-America selection.

Sheila was graduated from UCLA and was a member of the UCLA Bruin team that won the NCAA national titles in 1984 and 1982. She obtained a master's degree from USC, with a 3.96 grade point average. She is from Diamond Bar, CA.

Lisa Fernandez

Lisa, from Long Beach, CA is an energetic pitcher who makes headlines. During her years at UCLA, she helped lead the softball team to two NCAA Women's College World Series titles and was a four time NCAA All–American. During her senior year, she had an ERA of 0.51 *and* a batting average of .510, two records that are expected to be unchallenged for years.

The ASA named her "Sportswoman of the Year" in 1991 and again in 1992.

She pitched at Atlanta in 1996, and ended with an ERA of 0.33, held her opponents to a .111 batting average, allowed no walks, and had thirty–one strikeouts.

More recently, in the final (gold-medal) game against Australia at the South Pacific Classic in New Zealand, Lisa was perfect— no runs, no hits, no walks, no one got to first base. Lisa was a gold medalist at the 1999 Canada Cup, where her win/loss record was 3-0, with an ERA of 0.00 and forty strikeouts in 20.2 innings. With two triples, a home run, and four RBIs, she finished that championship series with a .348 batting average. She had the game-winning hit against the Canadian team at the 1999 Pan American Games, and was 3-0 again as a pitcher, with a no-hitter against Cuba.

Lori Harrigan

Lori, a pitcher, is a graduate of the University of Nevada-Las Vegas, where she holds UNLV records for wins (83), saves (7), strikeouts (725), ERA (0.77), complete games (123), shutouts (53), and innings pitched (1,034.6).

Being a member of gold-medal-winning international teams is something Lori has been doing since 1992 in China. At the 1996 Olympic Summer Games, she pitched a 4-0 complete game shutout of Chinese Taipei. Lori gave up two hits and struck out five. She ended the Games with an ERA of 0.00, tied with teammate Christa Williams.

More recently, she pitched a shutout (with nine strikeouts) against New Zealand to help the U.S. earn a gold medal at the 1998 South Pacific Classic, and she was a member of the 1998 Women's World Champions.

In 1999, Lori was a member of three USA teams that won gold medals. During the Canada Cup, she pitched 11.1

innings, saved a game, had fourteen strikeouts, walked one, and ended with an ERA of 0.62. At the Pan American Games, she pitched fourteen innings, struck out twenty-five, won two games, and had an ERA of 0.50. At the U.S. Olympic Cup games, Lori had a 3-2 win over Australia, allowed four hits and no walks, and recorded six strikeouts.

Danielle Henderson

Pitcher Danielle Henderson has finished her senior year at the University of Massachusetts, where she was an assistant coach and set NCAA and University of Massachusetts records for consecutive scoreless innings and winning streaks, respectively.

She has been a national participant at the 1998 and 1999 Coca-Cola USA Softball Women's National Team Festivals, but actually has more recent experience at international events.

She was 3-0 at the 1999 Canada Cup, had a 1.50 ERA, with twenty-eight strikeouts and two walks in fourteen innings. Danielle pitched two perfect games during the 1999 Pan American Games: seven innings against Colombia and five against the Bahamas. Over a span of seventeen innings, she allowed one hit and struck out forty-two. Her final gold medal for 1999 came at the U.S. Olympic Cup, where she shut out Canada on two hits, no walks, and sixteen strikeouts.

Jennifer McFalls

Jennifer was an alternate on the 1996 Olympic Summer Games softball team and made the roster for Sydney 2000. The former Texas A & M "Aggie" won gold medals at both the 1998 and 1999 Coca-Cola USA Softball Women's National Team Festivals.

On the international level, Jennifer was on the 1997 USA team that went 10-0 against China and Australia during the American Challenge Series. She was a member of both gold-medal teams—the ISF Women's World Championship and the South Pacific Classic—during 1998.

Jennifer played in three more medal-winning events in 1999: On the USA Gold Team at the Canada Cup, the U.S. Olympic Cup, and the Pan American Games. At the latter, she went four for six, drove in two runs, and scored six.

Stacey Nuveman

Stacey, a catcher on the 2000 Olympic Games roster, attends UCLA, where she played on the 1999 NCAA Softball National Championship team. She was also named PAC 10 Player of the Year, and was a first-team NFCA All-American, All-Pacific, and All-PAC 10.

Nationally, she was a silver medalist at the 1999 Coca-Cola USA Softball Women's Festival and a finalist for the 1999 AAU James E. Sullivan Award.

Stacey earned gold medals in 1999, too. At the Canada Cup, she ended with a .385 batting average, after hitting three home runs and a double. She had eight RBIs and scored five runs. At the Pan American Games, she again had three home runs and a double, while driving in seven runs and scoring six. Her batting average was .474. Her U.S. Olympic Cup championship game against Australia yielded a three-run homer, and Stacey finished the tournament with three hits and four RBIs.

Leah O'Brien-Amico

Outfielder Leah O'Brien-Amico is no stranger to Olympic Games competitions or other international events. Leah played in seven of the nine Olympic softball games in 1996, and had a .300 batting average and a no-errors performance in right field. She hit .200 and had one RBI during the 1997 American Challenge Series, then went on to a silver medal at Superball '97, where she batted .389.

Her home run and two RBIs at the South Pacific Classic led the USA to its fourth consecutive gold medal at the 1998 ISF Women's World Championships. She batted .343, had two doubles, one home run, and five RBIs. Leah accounted for all three of USA Gold's runs in its victory over Australia at the 1999 Canada Cup. For the Pan American Games, Leah hit .333, scored six runs, and had seven RBIs. Her hits included two triples and a double. The U.S. Olympic Cup games produced a .300 batting average, one RBI, two runs scored, and three hits.

Dot Richardson

Shortstop Dot Richardson began playing softball at ten when the Little League baseball team in her neighborhood told her to cut her hair and change her name to Bob if she wanted to play. Baseball's loss was softball's gain.

Dot has played on medal–winning teams since 1983 when she attended UCLA. She was the 1980s NCAA "Player of the Decade" and a four-time NCAA All–American.

Along the way, she completed medical school, finished her residency, and is now an orthopedic surgeon. Dot managed to do this while playing weekends for the Raybestos Brakettes in Connecticut. She kept her hitting skills up to par by installing a batting cage in her apartment.

One of several stars at Atlanta in 1996, Dot batted .273, had nine hits (including two doubles and three home runs), and seven RBIs. At the 1999 Canada Cup, Dot had eleven hits, including four home runs. One home run was a bases-loaded grand slam—a career first. She also hit a double, had eleven RBIs, scored nine runs, and was named the tournament's "Most Inspirational Player." Her gold-medal effort at the 1999 Pan American Games included two triples, two doubles, and a .342 batting average. Dot had a .333 batting average, with five hits, at the 1999 U.S. Olympic Cup, another gold-medal performance.

Michele Smith

In 1986, Michele's softball pitching days were nearly ended by a severe injury to the muscles and nerve endings in her left arm. Ten years later, she was in Atlanta with the rest of Team USA, where she played in every game, finished with an ERA of 1.50, and had twenty–three strikeouts. She had a 3-0 record at the 1999 Canada Cup, with an ERA of 0.47, and she bested this record at the 1999 Pan American Games, where she compiled a 4-0 record. The high point of that series was a shutout performance against Canada in the final game for the gold medal.

Michelle attended Oklahoma State University. By the time she graduated she and had pitched forty–six shutouts and compiled an 82–20 won–loss record.

Michele is no stranger to gold medals—she has been earning them regularly since 1993. That year, the ASA named her

"Sportswoman of the Year." Michele speaks fluent Japanese and was named MVP of the Japan League in 1994, an honor all by itself. She continued to play in the Japan League and was their again in 1997 and 1998.

Michelle Venturella

Michelle, a catcher from Indianapolis, IN, was an alternate at the 1996 Olympic Summer Games in Atlanta. She has played in the Big Ten and on the national level since 1992, and been a member of USA Softball teams that competed in the 1997 American Challenge Series, Superball '97, and the 1997 Pan American Qualifier.

In 1998, she was part of the gold medal teams that won the South Pacific Classic and the ISF World Championships. Team USA Blue finished third at the Canada Cup, where Michelle had a home run, a double, and two RBIs, and scored two runs. That same year, the USA Team won the U.S. Olympic Cup, and Michelle had a .333 batting average that included a double.

Christa Williams

Christa was only fifteen when the tryouts began for Team USA headed to Atlanta and had just been graduated from high school in 1996 when the Olympic Summer Games began. This youngest player on the U.S. team won two games at Atlanta, allowed no runs (0.00 ERA), and struck out fifteen. Christa was a pitcher for Team USA Blue at the 1999 Canada Cup, where her pitching record was 4-1. Two of the games were shutouts, and she struck out forty-one batters in 27.1 innings. She allowed only fifteen hits, had an ERA of 1.28, and received the Top Pitcher Award. Her gold-medal effort at the 1999 U.S. Olympic Cup was capped with a two-hitter against Australia in the final, championship game.

While playing one year for UCLA, Williams received the Mary Lou Retton Award from the USOC in 1995, recognition of her status as a "rising star" in her Olympic sport.

Alternates

Amanda Freed

Amanda Freed, a pitcher and alternate on the 2000 USA Softball Team, attends UCLA, where she led the Bruins to a second-place finish at the 2000 Women's College World Series. She was a three-time NFCA Player of the Week during the 2000 season, was named Most Outstanding Pitcher at the 2000 Paradise Softball Classic, and was the Most Valuable Pitcher at the 2000 USF-Louisville Slugger Tournament. Her academic achievements include a perfect GPA of 4.0.

Amanda has participated nationally since 1994. She was a silver medalist at the 1998 Coca-Cola USA Softball Women's National Team Festival, and she participated again in 1999.

In high school, Amanda earned twelve varsity letters—four each in softball, soccer, and volleyball.

Teri Klement-Goldberg

Teri Klement-Goldberg, an alternate utility player on the 2000 Olympic squad, played for Colorado State and is a former head coach at that university. She is Colorado's career leader in batting average (.383), hits (210), home runs (13), doubles (35), triples (11), runs (95), walks (48), RBIs (121), and slugging percentage (.557).

Teri has played at the national level since 1987, most recently winning a bronze medal at the 1999 Coca-Cola USA Softball Women's National Team Festival.

Internationally, Teri has played in Italy and Holland and was on the USA squad that won the 1997 Pan American Qualifier. There she had two triples and a home run, and scored thirteen runs, with a .465 batting average. She led the team with twenty hits, seven of them doubles, and eighteen RBIs. At the 1998 South Pacific Classic, she helped win a gold medal for the USA Team, then was named Top Hitter at the 1999 Canada Cup. As a member of team USA Blue, her on-base percentage was .528, with fifteen hits, four home runs, eleven runs scored, and ten RBIs. Teri finished 1999 as a gold medal-winner at the U.S. Olympic Cup.

Amanda Scott

Amanda Scott, a pitcher and alternate on the 2000 Softball Team, attends Fresno State, where she was an Academic All-American in 1998 and led the Bulldogs to the NCAA National Championship. That same year she was named Most Outstanding Player at the College World Series.

Nationally, Amanda was in the USA Softball National Team Festival at Midland, MI, where she had a 2-1 win/loss record and an ERA of 0.75. In 1998 she was a gold medalist at the Coca-Cola USA Softball National Team Festival. She was a silver medalist at the same Festival in 1999.

Amanda pitched internationally at the 1997 Pan American Games where she had a 2-0 win/loss record while chalking up thirteen strikeouts. Scott was part of both teams that won the ISF World Championship in 1998 and the Canada Cup in 1999. At the Canada Cup she had a 1-0 win/loss record, struck out six, scored one run, and had one RBI.

Shelly Stokes

Shelly was a member of the USA Team that won the gold medal at the 1996 Olympic Games, as well as of the USA Team that won the gold medal at the 1998 South Pacific Classic in Christchurch, New Zealand. A member of the 1998 ISF Women's World Championship team, Shelly had three doubles, a home run, four RBIs, and a .267 batting average. She continued with three hits and scored three runs at the Canada Cup in 1999, and contributed one home run, four RBIs, and a .308 batting average at the Pan American Games that same year.

At the national level, she played for the California Players of Bellflower, CA, who finished tied for fifth in the 1997 ASA Women's Major Fast-Pitch National Championship. She led the East squad to the gold medal at the 1997 USA Softball National Team Festival in Midland, MI, and was a member of the gold medal-winning North team at the 1995 U.S. Olympic Festival in Denver, CO.

Shelly is a former Fresno State University Bulldog catcher who went to the NCAA Women's College World Series all four years (1987-1990). Currently, she is a graduate assistant strength and conditioning coach at Fresno State University.

Dani Tyler

Dani Tyler, an alternate infielder at the 2000 Olympics, attended Drake University, where she was the 1996 Student-Athlete of the Year and where, in 1994 and 1995, she had the highest batting average on the team both years.

Dani has won silver and bronze medals on the national level: silver with the East squad at the 1997 USA Softball National Team Festival; silver at the 1999 Coca-Cola USA Softball Women's National Team Festival; and bronze at the 1998 Coca-Cola USA Softball Women's National Team Festival.

Internationally, Dani's medals have been mostly gold, beginning with the 1996 Olympic Summer Games. She was a member of the 1998 teams that won gold medals at the South Pacific Classic and the ISF World Championships. In 1999, she was a member of Team USA Blue that finished third at the Canada Cup, batting .250 with two doubles, three RBIs, and two runs scored.

Coaches

Ralph Raymond	Head coach
Margo Jonker	Assistant coach
Shirley Topley	Assistant coach

Ralph Raymond

A member of the Softball Hall of Fame, head coach Ralph Raymond has coached softball for over 30 years. The head coach of the gold medal 1999 Pan American Games team, the gold medal 1999 Canada Cup team, and the gold medal 1996 Olympic Games team, Raymond has also won the ISF World Championships five times, in the process compiling a winning streak of 61-0 in World Championship games.

Margo Jonker

An assistant coach for the teams that won both the 1999 Pan American Games gold medal and the 1999 Canada Cup gold medal, Margo Jonker also has been the head coach for the University of Central Michigan since 1979. While coaching college she has won nine Mid-American Conference titles and has been voted Mid-American Coach of the Year seven times.

Shirley Topley

Assistant coach Shirley Topley was elected to the National Softball Hall of Fame in 1981. During her career Shirley earned ASA All-America honors 11 times and participated in 16 national championships. Shirley helped coach the gold medal 1999 Pan American Games team, the Canada Cup winning team, and the 1996 Olympic Games gold medal winning team.

3

Getting Started

Softball—egalitarian almost from the beginning—was not limited to males, but was played by young girls and women, too, especially after it became an outdoor sport. Today, it is the third most popular collegiate sport for women; track and basketball are tied for first.

Finding a Team

Nearly 4.5 million players enjoy softball each season, with 60 divisions offering slow pitch, fast pitch, or modified pitch. With 260,000 registered teams in the United States, the ASA has organized a nationwide network of state and metropolitan organizations that can help anyone get started playing organized softball. For help locating a state commissioner in your area, contact the ASA at:

2801 N.E. 50th Street
Oklahoma City, OK 73111
Phone: (405) 424-5266
Fax: (405) 424-3855
Online: www.softball.org

The physical education department at a local school, the YMCA or YWCA, and a community's parks and recreation department are all possible contacts for anyone who wants to become a softball player—fast pitch, modified pitch, slow pitch, or 16-inch slow pitch.

Fast Pitch Softball

Olympic rules require that the ball be thrown by the pitcher underhanded, but with windmill-style delivery. Before the pitcher delivers the pitch, both feet must be on the ground and inside the length of the pitcher's plate. For men, the pivot foot must contact the pitcher's plate and the non–pivot foot can be on or behind the plate. For women, both feet must be in contact with the pitcher's plate.

Next, the pitcher takes a signal from the catcher, holds the ball in both hands—but not for longer than 10 seconds—and is certain that the catcher is in position. As soon as one hand is taken off the ball, the pitch begins. Pitchers are not allowed to change their minds once the pitch begins.

Bases are 60 feet apart, there are three outfielders, and the pitcher is 40 feet from home plate in the women's game; 46 feet from home plate in the men's game. Outfield fences have minimum and maximum distances of 200 and 250 feet for women; 225 and 250 feet for men.

Fast pitch softball games usually feature strong pitchers, and as a result, are often low-scoring pitching duels.

Modified Pitch Softball

Modified pitch is similar to fast pitch—the distance between bases and the distance from the pitcher's plate to the batter's box are the same as described above. The difference is that all modified pitch softball pitchers, male and female, must have both feet on the ground and within the length of the pitcher's plate when pitching; when releasing the ball, their hips must be square to home plate. No windmill or slingshot delivery is allowed. Unlike fast pitch, with its minimum and maximum distances to the outfield fence, there is only a minimum distance for modified pitch: 200 feet for women; 265 feet for men.

ASA/USA Softball

Taking her cut. Women's slow pitch

Slow Pitch Softball

Slow pitch teams have 10 players, with the extra player allowed to roam the area between the infield and outfield. He or she can be a "short fielder" as opposed to an infielder, or the extra player can be used as the fourth outfielder.

In this version, the bases are 65 feet apart, and the pitcher is 50 feet from home plate. Outfield fences range in distance from 265 feet to a maximum of 300 feet.

Slow pitch uses the standard 12–inch ball, but it is pitched in an arc between 6 feet and 12 feet. That makes it an "easy" target for hitters, and consequently, these games are often high-scoring events. Players may not bunt or steal bases and must remain on base until the ball reaches home plate.

ASA/USA Softball
Ready to launch one. Girls' slow pitch

16-Inch Slow Pitch

Sixteen-inch slow pitch softball uses a white ball with white stitching that is 15-7/8 inches to 16-1/8 inches in circumference. It has a minimum weight of 9 ounces and a maximum weight of 10 ounces. The bases are 55 feet apart and the distance from the pitcher's plate to home plate is 38 feet for both men's and women's teams. Runners can lead off and be called out if touched while off a base; pitchers can fake once to the batter and attempt a pickoff of the runner, but the runner cannot advance unless the pitched ball is hit. Only the fence distances are different: 200 feet for women and 250 feet for men.

The Equipment

As a general rule, the quality of softball equipment purchased should be based on how often the athlete will play. Several games per week, along with high interest on the part of the player, will required durable, high-quality (and more expensive) equipment. Beginning players, perhaps with lower interest and fewer games per week, will need less durable, lower-quality (and less expensive) equipment.

All equipment should be "official," which means that it meets the ASA specifications governing bats, spikes/cleats on shoes, gloves and mitts, balls, and protective equipment. Players, especially fast-pitch catchers, should wear their gear during practices, as well as during games, for protection and to become comfortable with the fit.

One final consideration is where the softball games will be played. Dirt, grass, and asphalt require slightly different equipment. Plastic or rubber cleats are best for running on dirt or grass, while athletic shoes with thick soles are best for asphalt or concrete.

Softballs

The International Joint Rules Committee of the International Softball Federation (ISF) sets the standards for softballs internationally, and the ASA sets the standards nationally. Balls may vary in circumference by 1/4 of an inch—from 11-7/8 inches to 12-1/8 inches—and may vary by 3/4 of an ounce in weight—6-1/4 ounces to 7 ounces. The cover must either be horsehide or cowhide, pebble-textured, with stitching similar to a baseball.

In Olympic fast-pitch competitions, softballs must be white and of a flat-seam style with at least 88 white stitches. The 12-inch ball is also used for men's and women's fast pitch, and boys and girls 12-, 14-, 16-, and 18-under fast pitch. Adult males and boys 14-, 16-, and 18-under use the 12-inch ball for slow pitch.

An 11-inch ball with white stitching is used for girls and boys ages 10 and under playing fast pitch softball. An 11-inch ball with red stitching is used for slow pitch softball played by girls 12-, 14-, 16-, and 18-under. Boys in the 10- and 12-under category of slow pitch also use an 11-inch ball with red stitching. This ball is used for either slow pitch or fast pitch and has a minimum circumference of 10-7/8 inches; a maximum of 11-1/8 inches, and weighs between 5-7/8 ounces and 6-1/8 ounces.

Bats

Official bats are constructed from a single piece of hardwood with the grain of the wood running parallel. Bats made from metal, plastic, an aluminum alloy, or other man-made materials are acceptable as well. Bats cannot be longer than 34 inches or weigh more than 38 ounces. (Bats for young, beginning players are shorter and lighter.) A bat's diameter cannot exceed 2-1/4 inches at its thickest part.

Metal bats must meet similar requirements. All bats, whether wood or metal, require a safety grip (10 to 15 inches long) and an "Official Softball" label.

ASA/USA Softball

Bird's-eye view. Men's fast pitch

When purchasing a bat, its grip, weight, and length are the important considerations. Small hands need a narrow handle;

large hands a thicker handle, depending on how the bat is held. Practicing with different handles will help to determine which bat to purchase. Some players wear batting gloves to serve as shock absorbers and to get a better grip on the bat. They may also help to prevent blisters and calluses.

A simple weight test is to take the bat in one hand, hold the bat straight out, and keep it steady and parallel to the ground. If the player can do this for 10 seconds without stress or fatigue, that is probably the best weight. A heavy bat is more powerful, but if it's too heavy for the player to swing comfortably, there's no advantage from the extra weight. In fact, the wrong weight may interfere with a player's timing.

The right length helps the player to hit the ball with the fat part of the bat and should suit a player's stance. Long bats seem to work well for players who stand back from the plate; shorter bats seem to be the choice of players who "crowd" the plate (stand closer to the plate).

Warm-up bats must be labeled clearly with the words, "warm-up bat" or the initials "WB."

Mitts and Gloves

Softball mitts are shaped like winter mittens, except they are bigger and made of leather. A catcher's mitt has thick padding and is almost a circular shape. A first baseman's mitt is more flexible, with a larger pocket area, and often is used by catchers. The softball rules allow catchers and first basemen to wear fielder's gloves, but fielders cannot wear mitts. Most fielders wear a glove with three or four finger sections, plus one for the thumb. Lacing and webbing between finger and thumb sections cannot be longer than 5 inches.

When trying on a new glove, try to shape it and see if the pocket is comfortable. If it is and the price is right, that's probably the glove to buy. "Signature" gloves can be alluring, but usually only add to the cost, not the comfort.

New leather gloves are stiff and need breaking in. There are many methods. Leather softening products for new gloves are available. The area to be shaped can be pounded with a fist. You can wrap the glove around a ball, secure it with rubber bands, and let it sit for a period of time. Using the glove to play catch (or softball) is another way of breaking it in.

ASA/USA Softball
Boys' 16-under slow pitch at ASA 1997 National Tournament

Shoes

Uppers made of leather, nylon, canvas, or other approved materials are available. Some have padded tongues, Achilles heel guards, and arch supports. Higher quality will, of course, mean higher price. Buy shoes suited to the playing field.

Softball shoes may have soft or hard rubber cleats on the soles. Metal sole or heel plates are acceptable, but the spikes must not be longer than 3/4 inch. They cannot screw onto a post, but can screw into a shoe. They are not legal for youths at any level or style of softball play.

Protective Equipment

The catcher wears more gear than any other player: a mask, throat protector, helmet, body protector, and shin guards.

Masks are lightweight, and have two padded bars and an attached throat protector. One bar rests on the forehead, the other on the chin. The large area in between should give the catcher a clear view of the players and field. If the catcher wears glasses, the mask should not catch on eyeglass frames.

Body protectors have straps that adjust for a secure, comfortable fit. Shin guards are required protective equipment and can prevent bruises and other injuries. For female catchers, there are body protectors with breast protectors attached, or the protectors may be sewn on. The extra width of these protectors may hamper throwing and restrict movement. Comfortable sports bras are available at department stores and sporting goods stores.

Junior Olympic slow pitch catchers *must* wear a batter's helmet with ear flaps, or a catcher's helmet and mask, with an optional throat protector.

Junior Olympic fast pitch catchers *must* wear all the protective gear. The only options are an attached throat protector or an extended wire throat protector.

Offensive fast pitch players must wear helmets with double ear flaps for batting, while in the on-deck circle waiting to bat, and when on base. Helmets are allowed for defensive players, and any player (offensive or defensive) may wear an approved plastic face mask.

Uniforms

Uniforms range from T-shirts and gym shorts worn with knee socks to regular baseball/softball-style shirts and knickers with knee socks. Some players add sliding pads or wear special sliding pants. A baseball cap protects eyes from the sun, keeps hair under control, and is required for all players. Headbands and visors are legal wear, but must be worn properly, *e.g.,* not dangling around the neck. Regardless of the uniform choice, all players must wear the same color and style.

Other Equipment

Not all teams play on softball diamonds that are well-maintained and ready for games. Teams may need to purchase a home plate, pitcher's plate, and a set of bases, with the stakes to drive them into the ground. Don't use a bat for this job; have a hammer handy. Teams may, at times, have to "lay out" the infield, so a 100-foot tape measure is a good purchase.

Care of Equipment

Bats

Wipe off dirt and mud with a damp cloth. Inspect the bat for cracks because cracked bats are dangerous—they can come apart and send pieces flying. Check the wear on safety grips and replace as needed.

Mitts and Gloves

They get dirty, but can be wiped with a damp cloth to clean.

Then rub in some neat's-foot oil (available at sporting goods stores). With regular care, gloves and mitts will last longer, won't dry out and crack, and will resist scuff marks.

Shoes

If they are made of leather, clean and polish them. Also, remove dirt and grass from the cleats.

Protective Equipment

Check elastic straps for wear and stretch. Replace when necessary. Body protectors gather dust and should be beaten to remove it. A mask can be washed with warm water and soap, and straps and bars are replaceable when they become worn. Dirt wipes off shin and leg guards, and straps can be replaced as necessary.

Uniforms

With today's easy-care fabrics and wide selection of detergents and stain removers, regular washing should maintain a uniform's useful life.

4

Playing Softball

Softball is the fastest-growing seasonal sport, with millions of players from kids under 10 to seniors over 65 playing the game every year. They have found a game that provides exercise, builds friendships, and offers hours of fun.

The Playing Field

The softball playing field has the same outlines as those used in baseball, except the distance between the base paths for fast pitch and modified pitch is 60 feet rather than 90. In 16-inch and slow pitch, the distances are 55 feet and 65 feet, respectively. This gives softball players nearly one-third less distance than baseball players to work in, and they must react far more quickly. Distances from the pitcher to home plate and to the outfield fence are correspondingly shorter.

There is no pitcher's mound or elevation. Instead, the pitcher works from a pitching rubber, or pitcher's plate, within a circle with a radius of 8 feet. The distance from the rubber to home plate is 46 feet in men's fast pitch and modified pitch softball, and 40 feet in women's fast pitch and modified pitch. Fifty feet is the standard for slow pitch, and 38 feet for 16-inch pitch.

For youth fast pitch or slow pitch softball, the distance between bases, the distance from the pitcher to home plate, and the distance to the outfield are correspondingly shorter.

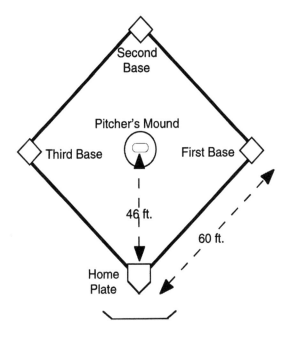

The infield area is named a diamond because of its shape, with home plate, and first, second, and third bases at the "points" of the diamond. Running along the first- and third-base lines to the left and right are the foul lines. Ground balls that hit first or third base and bounce over into foul territory are fair balls and playable. Balls hit in the air between the lines are fair; balls hit outside the lines are foul. Fly balls are fair and "in play" and playable when hit between these lines. Umpires need excellent vision to call these hits correctly, and at some games there will be umpires along the foul lines just for this purpose.

The outfield fences for women's fast, modified, and 16-inch softball are set at a minimum radius of 200 feet from home plate. Women's slow pitch uses 265 feet. Minimum distances for men range from 225 feet (fast pitch), 250 feet (16-inch), 265 feet (modified pitch), and 275 feet (slow pitch).

Within this area are the left, center, and right fielders. The short area between second and third bases and the outfield is covered by the shortstop position.

Home plate has a batter's box on each side. To the right and left of home plate is an "on deck circle," where the next batter waits his turn at bat.

Positions

A fast pitch softball team comprises nine players: pitcher, catcher, first, second, and third basemen, shortstop, and left, center, and right fielders. (There are ten players on a slow pitch team, with the tenth covering the area behind second and third bases and the left and center outfields.) The catcher crouches behind the plate, and the umpire is behind.

Outfielders

Outfielders do more than catch fly balls; there's always something for them to do. They must be aware and ready to run backward or forward as soon as the ball is pitched. Often, the sound of a solidly hit ball lets the outfielder know how to react. They need speed to cover their areas, the ability to catch fly balls, and accurate throwing. This accuracy must be done with strength, distance, and very little bounce on the ball when thrown to an infielder.

Outfielders must learn to make the adjustments needed when running to catch a fly ball or running to make a play on a ground ball hit through the infield. They must judge how the play will affect base runners and scoring opportunities for the offensive team. With experience, outfielders learn how the ball's flight is influenced by wind speed and direction, and adjust accordingly.

Outfielders learn to "call" for the catch or defer to another outfielder by saying, "Yours," or other appropriate words. The

ASA/USA Softball/Doug Hoke

Turning the double play. Girls' fast pitch

right fielder is the backup for any balls that are overthrown to first base and is the outfielder who throws to first to force out a hitter.

The center fielder often backs up the other outfielders. All three should be alert and aware of the game that is being played. Daydreaming can be costly.

Infielders

Infielders need to be agile and have good reflexes. They must be able to catch thrown balls, especially at first base, but they also need to know which balls to make a play on and which to leave for other players.

First basemen should have basic skills fielding ground balls, and the ability to run after foul balls along the first-base foul line, to run under pop-ups, and to field bunts. The ability to move the feet, stretch, and be a good target are additional skill needs. Left-handed first basemen have an advantage: they can throw more easily to the left side of the diamond.

They must react to where balls are hit and be ready to take throws from the other infielders—pitcher, catcher, second and third basemen, shortstop—and the right fielder.

Making the tag. Boys' slow pitch

They must "tag" offensive players or be prepared to "flip" (throw underhanded) a fielded ball to the second baseman or pitcher to make the play.

Second basemen and shortstops work as a team within the team, handling the infield's defense around second base, backing up each other on throws, and being part of a relay when balls are thrown from the outfield. They cover a lot of territory and need good, sure hands and the ability to "feed" or "flip" the ball to one another and other infielders.

They trade off duties depending on where balls are hit. For example, when balls are hit to the right side of the infield, the second baseman fields the ball or is the backup for the pitcher or first baseman, and the shortstop covers second base. When balls are hit to the left side of the infield, the shortstop makes the play or backs up the third baseman or pitcher, and the second baseman covers second.

The second baseman or shortstop (sometimes both) will be part of double plays—one of the exciting defensive moments in softball.

The third baseman covers the "hot" corner and has to be quick, have a strong arm, and be totally unafraid of and unflinching with any balls hit his way.

Catcher

Catchers need wide-angle vision because they see the entire field and where all players are, both for their team and the opposition's base runners. They must be alert and aware, with the ability to throw accurately to other infielders, including the pitcher. A catcher needs a strong throwing arm.

Catchers try to keep base runners from "stealing" a base by "picking" them off. They must be prepared to receive balls thrown to home plate from the outfield and be ready to tag the runner out at home.

A catcher needs strong legs to squat and then take a semi-crouch position to receive the pitch. She needs size and strength, especially in the legs and upper body. The ball's target is the catcher's mitt, and the catcher must return the ball to the pitcher if the batter does not get a hit or a walk. The catcher fields bunts in front of home plate and must react rapidly to field the ball. The catcher defends home plate when runners try to score and backs up first and third basemen on ground balls. If the third baseman fields a bunt, the catcher covers third base. When pop-ups are in foul territory near home plate, they are the catcher's responsibility.

Catcher and pitcher are a team and work with their coach on signals and strategy. The catcher warms up the pitcher, discusses strategy for the game, and helps the pitcher to stay focused. A catcher who plays regularly with one pitcher can notice changes that may influence the pitcher's effectiveness.

The catcher, with her wide-angle view of the game, is the defensive leader who positions fielders and calls infield plays.

Pitcher

A pitcher must have consistent throwing ability and spends hours throwing a ball to develop speed and control. In fast pitch softball, that means getting the ball in the strike zone. Since batters are not all the same height, it is crucial to pitchers' success—and to the success of their teams—that pitchers have control and accuracy. Pitchers must have control of their emotions as well as the ball and not get upset easily.

They need strong legs, backs, and arms and the endurance to last full games and those with extra innings. The pitcher must want to be a pitcher and commit to a training schedule that maintains fitness and health.

Pitchers back up throws to home plate and third base and sometimes at first base. They need to be ready to field bunts and pop-ups, if necessary, and ground balls hit to the pitcher's area.

Like catchers, pitchers need to check that everyone is ready to play, be aware of where base runners are, know how many players are out, and know which batters are coming up to bat.

A Few Fundamentals

Youngsters new to the game of softball will be taught the fundamentals of play by their coach or his assistants. These include gripping the ball, catching and throwing it, running the bases, batting, and fielding ground or fly balls.

Coming home. Women's fast pitch

Gripping the Ball

Grips vary depending on the size of a player's hands. Young beginners, who have the smallest hands, use a four-finger grip. The two- or three-finger grips suit youths and adults with more developed hands, fingers, and wrists. Fingers hold the ball—always across the seams—and not in the palm of the hand. This allows for good wrist action, with the thumb underneath the ball and the little finger used to guide and support the ball. (For a two-finger grip, the thumb is underneath and the ring and little fingers are alongside.)

Catching

To practice catching, a player needs a partner. They should stand 15 to 20 feet apart and throw the ball overhand to one another, while wearing a glove—on the left hand for throwing with the right hand and on the right hand for throwing with the left hand. Players should practice throwing and catching the ball above and below the waist, and include both practice backing up and moving forward to catch. As timing and skill improve and confidence increases, the players should move farther apart. The thrower needs to step into a throw and then let his arm complete the throwing motion after the ball is released.

For above the waist catches, the fingers of the glove should point up; for below the waist catches, the fingers of the glove should point down. The objective is to catch the ball in the pocket of the glove, bring the throwing hand in to grasp the ball, and throw it back. Players look at the ball as it approaches and catch it with both hands. Then, they are ready sooner to return the throw.

Enthusiastic youngsters should be cautioned to pay attention to the other players who are practicing, and never throw a ball until their partner is ready to receive it. The two should work out a "ready" signal ahead of time.

Running the Bases

When the ball is hit, complete (follow through on) the swing, drop the bat (never throw it), and run as fast as possible from home plate to first base. Players run in a straight line on the balls of the feet, but have their bodies relaxed and arms pumping. They look where they are running—to first base—touch the front of the base (the part nearest the leading foot) and run past the base. A part of good base running is listening to instructions from the first- and third-base coaches instead of watching the ball. This allows the player to concentrate on running.

Batting

Grip, stance, and swing are batting's three interrelated parts. The bat should be gripped with the fingers, not the palm of the hand. For right-handed batters, the left fingers of the left hand should curl around the bat and just touch the knob end. The right hand and fingers go above the left. Reverse the hand and finger order for left-handed batters. All players adjust the position of their hands and fingers to get a grip that is comfortable for them.

The batter stands in the batter's box, feet parallel to home plate, but with the front foot toward the pitcher. The chin rests on the front shoulder, the head is steady, and eyes are on the ball. The bat is not on the shoulder, but held away at about a 45° angle. Elbows are bent so the hands are near armpit height. Hips should be level, the knees bent a bit, and the weight on the balls of the feet.

The batter watches the ball, strides into the swing, brings the bat down from the shoulder, and hits the ball. The swing is completed by bringing the bat through the swing (the follow-through), so the bat touches the hitter's back on the left side, and the chin touches the right shoulder. Finally, the player drops the bat and sprints for first base.

As timing and concentration improve, batters become better hitters.

Fielding Ground Balls and Fly Balls

When fielding ground balls and fly balls, the player's feet should be spread and the fielder should be "square" to the batter. The body should be semi-crouched, knees bent, and weight on the balls of the feet. The heels barely touch the ground, and the hands should be in front of the player.

When the ball is hit and it's the infielder's play, she keeps her eyes on the ball and her body low to the ground. Both hands should reach out, with the glove hand low and almost touching the ground while the fielder moves forward to let the ball roll into her glove. Then, she grasps the ball with the throwing hand and completes the play.

When the play is to an outfielder, she keeps her eyes on the ball, but runs as fast as necessary to where she can catch the ball and complete or continue the play.

Playing the Game

A regulation softball game has nine players, is seven innings long, and is scored the same as baseball—runners move around the bases from first base to home plate. Every time a runner crosses home plate, that's one run for the team.

Each player has two roles—offense and defense. When your team is at bat in its half of an inning, you are on offense; when the other team is at bat, you are on defense. The object in every inning is to score runs (offense) or to keep your opponents from scoring (defense).

One inning is the length of time the defensive team has to prevent three players on the offensive team from getting hits or getting on base by other means. Three outs in an inning equal one try for a team.

Defensive players take their usual playing positions on the field at the top (or start) of the first inning. They are:

- *Pitcher:* Feet touching the pitcher's rubber or plate. (There is no pitcher's mound in softball.) When a game begins, the pitcher "presents the ball" by having both feet on the ground and contacting the pitcher's plate. The ball is held in front of the body (in both hands) for up to 20 seconds.

- *Catcher:* Crouched down, just behind the batter's box.
- *Center Fielder:* Standing in center field so that he can see the batter and the pitch when it is thrown.
- *Left Fielder and Right Fielder:* In from their respective foul lines—25 to 30 feet—depending on their knowledge of the batter's skill and tendencies.
- *First and Third Base:* Both begin by standing 5 to 6 feet in from the right or left foul lines, respectively, and 2 to 3 feet toward home plate.
- *Second Base and Shortstop:* The second baseman is to the right of second base, the shortstop to the left.

The umpire is behind the catcher and calls the balls, strikes, outs, and safes. He interprets the rules, resolves all disputes, and gives the traditional signal for the game to begin:

"Play Ball!"

Getting into position to score a run means getting on base. This can be accomplished in several different ways by the offensive team:

- The pitcher throws four pitches that are not in the batter's strike zone—in fast pitch, the area between a batter's armpits and the top of his knees; in slow pitch, the space over home plate that is between the batter's armpits and the front knee. This is a "walk," and the player goes to first base.
- The pitcher throws a ball that hits the batter, who goes to first base, but is not credited with a base hit.
- The batter hits the ball along the ground in fair territory and runs to first base before an infielder throws the ball to the player covering first. The batter becomes a

base runner. If he doesn't run fast enough and the ball arrives before he does, he is "out" for that inning.

- The batter hits the ball to the outfield where it may drop before an outfielder can reach it. If possible, the batter may run safely to second or third base, gaining a "double" or "triple." Otherwise, he is credited with a "single." If the ball is caught before hitting the ground, the hitter is out for that inning.

- The batter hits the ball so long and up in the air that no one is able to catch it, except perhaps a fan in the stands. This is an automatic home run, but the hitter must be sure to touch all three bases and home plate to earn it.

- All players on base advance as their teammates get hits or get on base. Coaching strategy sometimes dictates that a hitter be allowed to gain first base when the ball he hits is fielded by a defender, and an out is made at second or third base instead.

- If a defender makes an error, this may enable a hitter to gain first base.

A designated hitter is allowed as long as his name was on the official lineup sheet and he remains in the same batting order during the game. If a pinch-hitter or pinch-runner replaces the designated hitter, he may not return a second time. The designated hitter is not allowed to play defense.

A starting player is allowed to reenter the game one time, if another player has substituted for him, but he must return to his original batting spot.

The defensive (or fielding) team tries to stop the offensive (hitting) team from scoring runs by:

- Catching fly balls to the outfield, either in fair or foul territory.

- Catching "pop-up" fly balls to the infield.

- Fielding an infield ground ball and throwing to first base before the hitter gets there.

- A base runner tries to "steal" the next base and is caught off base and tagged with the ball.

- A base runner tries to advance on a ground ball but is "forced out" when an infielder with the ball touches the base he is running to.

- A base runner tries to advance on a fly ball and is caught off base and tagged with the ball.

- The pitcher "strikes out" the hitter.

If a game is tied at the end of regulation play, the game continues until one team scores more runs than the other in a complete inning; or, if the home team, batting in the second half of an inning, scores enough runs to win before the third out.

Keeping Score

More than recording hits, runs, errors, and the name of the winning pitcher, the scorekeeper for a softball game must know the rules of the game and how to record the results of each at-bat. Score sheets list each player by uniform number, name, and position in the batting order for the game. Positions are numbered, traditionally, from the pitcher to the short fielder (in slow pitch).

Player	Position
Pitcher	No. 1
Catcher	No. 2
First baseman	No. 3
Second baseman	No. 4
Third baseman	No. 5
Shortstop	No. 6
Left fielder	No. 7

Center fielder	No. 8
Right fielder	No. 9
Short fielder	No. 10*
	*(slow pitch only)

The scorer uses symbols that simplify his record keeping of all the plays, yet they are easily understood. A few of the common symbols are:

Play	Symbol
Assist	A
Base on balls	BB
Double	2B
Double play	DP
Error (fielding)	E
Flyout	F
Home run	HR
Infield fly	IF
Intentional walk	IBB
Putout	PO
Single	1B
Strikeout (called)	KC
Strikeout (swinging)	K
Triple	3B
At bat	AB
Run	R
Hit	H
Runs batted in	RBI
Strikeouts	SO

Scorers decide whether an error or a hit allows a player to get to first base. However, they never overrule umpires or breach the official rules.

Under ASA rules, batting and fielding records (times at bat, runs scored, base hits, putouts, assists, and errors) must be kept for each player in the game.

If a pitcher has pitched four innings but is replaced while his team is ahead, he is the winning pitcher. But, his team must remain ahead to the end of the game.

If a pitcher is replaced while his team is losing, and his team does not tie the score or win the game, he is the losing pitcher. The number of innings he has pitched is irrelevant.

Mental Softball

Gymnasts and figure skaters visualize their routines and programs before competing, and this same visualization practice is just as valuable for the softball player.

All hitters—those in the regular lineup as well as those who pinch hit—can benefit by watching the ball and expecting to hit it. This inner confidence can transform itself into batting confidence, for the "power of positive thinking," although a cliché, does work.

Pitchers have to picture the strike zone and be able to visualize throwing the ball within that unmarked area. They need to block out distractions and concentrate. Especially important to a pitcher is the leadoff hitter, for he often determines how the inning progresses.

Base runners can imagine mental pictures of running the bases in different situations, *e.g.*, the team is way behind or far ahead; the score is tied; or there is a runner, or runners, on base ahead of the runner. Runners should keep their minds and memories focused on the game—what inning it is, current number of outs, and the score—and run according to the situation.

Whether playing infield or outfield, players can picture the ball coming to them for the play or as the backup. Mentally rehearse where the ball should go if there are runners on base and which bases they are on. Just the same as an offensive player, the mind and memory should be "in the game," always aware of the inning, outs, and score.

Rules to Remember

- Unsportsmanlike conduct—insults to the opposition, any official, or fans—is forbidden. For a player, this means instant ejection from the game, although he may stay on the bench. If the unsportsmanlike behavior continues, the player must go to the dressing room or leave the field. Ignoring these directions will cause a forfeit of the game.

- A coach may be given a warning for a first unsportsmanlike offense. He is ejected if there is a second.

- First and third base coaches stay in their coaching boxes.

- The dugout area is for coaches, players, substitutes, and other people associated with the game. This is where they remain unless the rules or the umpire allow them to be outside that area. The team is warned the first time this rule is disobeyed. After that, the team member is ejected.

- No foreign substance can be used on the ball. If this rule is ignored, the player should be ejected.

- Pitchers cannot wear a batting glove on their pitching hand, tape on fingers, or anything (jewelry, watch, sweat band) on the wrist or forearm. A first offense results in an illegal-pitch call.

UMPIRE SIGNAL CHART

INFIELD FLY
Raise right arm with fist closed.
Verbally call, "Infield Fly."

FAIR BALL
Point towards fair ground with
hand closest to infield. No verbal
call.

FOUL BALL
First give DEAD BALL signal.
Verbally call, "Foul Ball."

PLAY BALL
Motion with either hand to the
pitcher. Verbally call, "Play Ball."

TIME/DEAD BALL
Raise both hands with open
palms away from the body.
Verbally call, "Time" or "Dead
Ball."

COUNT
Raise both arms up, indicate
strikes with fingers on right hand
and balls with fingers on left
hand. Verbally give count. Use
consecutive fingers when giving
count.

STRIKE/OUT
Bring left arm with hand closed to
midsection as right arm is
extended straight up with hand
facing ear. Then pull down at
elbow while closing fist. Verbally
call, "Strike" or "Out."

5

ASA Programs

Over the last 60 years, the ASA (also known as USA Softball) has worked tirelessly with softball players to help them upgrade their skills. The organization has developed extensive training programs for coaches and umpires, and supervises a wide network of competitions, championships, tournaments, and programs.

International Competitions

As the National Governing Body (NGB) for amateur softball in the United States, the ASA works with the USOC to select and train the athletes who represent the United States in international competitions—the World Championships, the Pan American Games, and the Summer Olympic Games. There are four divisions for national teams: women, men, junior women (18-under), and junior men. Then, every four years, each division plays in a world championship. USA women won the World Championship in 1986, 1990, 1994, and a record-setting fourth title in 1998. They won gold at the 1979, 1987, 1991, 1995, and 1999 Pan American Games. (Their silver medal year was 1983.) USA men have five World Championship titles and six silver medals at the Pan American Games—1979, 1983, 1987, 1991, 1995, and 1999. At the 1997 ISF Junior Men's World Championships, the

American men did not medal. The USA Junior Women's Team won its World Championship in 1995 by dominating the field with 15 straight shutouts.

ASA/USA Softball

The ecstasy of winning it all! We're No.1! Girls' fast pitch

Championships and Tournaments

In addition to its international responsibilities, the ASA conducts more than 60 national championships in slow, fast, and modified pitch softball. Teams work their way through qualifying tournaments during the season, and one team in each division earns a national championship. Only 1 percent of teams playing each season are good enough to make it to an ASA National Championship.

The large network of state and metro associations belonging to the ASA hold tournaments and local league games with more than 4 million players participating each year.

ASA/USA Softball
The agony of defeat – second-place finisher at ASA Nationals

Junior Olympic Program

The Junior Olympic Program (JOP) is the ASA softball program for all youth ages 18 and under. Emphasis is on building self-confidence and a healthy attitude, while participants learn new skills, improve old ones, make new friends, and have fun. Winning is not overemphasized.

There are five age divisions: 18-under, 16-under, 14-under, 12-under, and 10-under, with fast pitch and slow pitch softball offered both for girls and boys. Players participate at skill classification levels and move up as their skills improve. This means everyone plays competitively, and a youngster need not be a "star" to make the team.

The JOP holds national championships for girls and boys in both fast and slow pitch. Some 10,000 boys and girls participate in these games which, beginning in 1997, named first-, second-, and third-team All-Americans.

By 1996, the JOP had 78,000 teams, with 1.2 million players and 300,000 coaches. ASA youth programs have been the path to college scholarships for many. In 1997 nearly 80 percent of NCAA Division I players came from the ASA JO summer programs, and 13 of the 15 players on the 1996 gold medal team at Atlanta started out in the JOP.

Volunteer Improvement Program (VIP)

Most coaches are volunteers. In 1987 the ASA recognized this and began a certification program that prepares coaches to coach and to develop the skills of their players. National coaching schools are held every year and offer coaching education for all levels of softball. They also help coaches to upgrade their skills to current requirements. There are 6,000 coaches enrolled in the VIP, and nearly 2,000 attend Level I and II schools each year.

Beginning coaches are encouraged to attend a Level I National Coaching School, after which they are automatically certified at the Bronze 1 Level and may progress to Levels 2, 3, and 4. Certification at the silver and gold levels is next, if desired. Level II National Coaching Schools are for coaches with more advanced players who are working to attain their next skill level.

The ASA has many resources for coaches, including a set of eight tapes that demonstrate fundamental softball skills and techniques. There are videos on pitching, defense, hitting, strategies for the game, and training programs.

ASA/USA Softball

**Safe at home. NCAA National Championship
at ASA Hall of Fame Stadium in Oklahoma City**

Program for Umpires

Umpires receive extensive training from the ASA and attend National Umpire Schools, plus there are rules and mechanics schools at local, state, and regional levels. Of the more than 56,000 registered ASA umpires each year, 13 percent are female.

Training materials—videos, books, slides, and cassette tapes—are available from the ASA for those unable to attend schools. Once certification is received from the ISF (an honor), umpires are eligible to work as the U.S. representative for ISF-sanctioned World Championships, the Pan American Games and the Olympic Games. In fact, at Atlanta, all the umpires were ASA trained.

ASA/USA Softball

Over 13 percent of the ASA's more than 56,000 umpires
are women.

Other ASA Programs

The ASA/USA Softball organization sponsors several other
programs that provide individual instruction for athletes and
promote amateur softball nationally and internationally.

National Teams and Elite Athlete Programs

With the USOC, the ASA works to select and prepare the softball teams that represent the United States in international competitions. Their elite athlete programs offer team camps and many opportunities for softball players to represent the United States on a national level. Athletes are eligible for training grants and awards through the USOC, and many participate in clinics and make personal appearances.

Yearly Camps

In addition to team camps for the four divisions of national teams, there are National Team Camps, where players from around the United States compete against one another. These are excellent opportunities to be evaluated and selected, perhaps, as a member of a U.S. team preparing for an international competition.

A four-day ASA/USA Softball Championship Player Camp is offered each year in Oklahoma for softball players who played in a recent ASA/USA Softball National Championship. Participants must be 13 to 18 years old, and the camp is open to "commuters" or those from out of the area who would stay overnight. The schedule at this camp covers a range of instruction from conditioning to actually playing softball games. Participants receive hitting instruction as well as work on relays, cut-offs, game situations, and basic drills. The instructors are established coaches from the college level with assistance from local athletes. Individual attention is provided, and an added benefit is the opportunity to earn a college scholarship.

In 1997, ASA/USA Softball started Softball Elite Hitting Camps, which cover all aspects of the game, but emphasize hitting. Offense, defense, and fundamentals are stressed as well. Fast pitch softball is the focus, but slow pitch players can improve their skills as well. Boys and girls from 9 to 17 are welcome at these day camps, which are conducted by an outstanding staff of coaches and assistants. Lisa Fernandez, Jennifer Brundage, and Laura Berg, members of the 1996 and 2000 Olympic teams, were assistants in 1997.

New ASA Programs

After Atlanta, the ASA began two programs—the USA Softball National Team Festival and the American Challenge Series. The Festival was first held in 1997 and showcased the top 60 women fast-pitch players. Many of them were U.S. gold medalists from World Championship, Pan American, and Olympic games. The Festival is part of the selection process for the USA softball team that competed in the 2000 games at Sydney. The men's program also initiated a festival in 1998.

The Challenge Series was first held in 1997 and was a competition among the three medal-winning teams at Atlanta: the U.S., China, and Australia. As an annual event, U.S. women softball players are prepared to challenge the rest of the world and promote the sport to the general public.

6

Health and Fitness

Good health and physical fitness are necessary for anyone who competes in any sport. A major fringe benefit of softball is that the fitness you develop while learning and training for that sport will carry over to any other sports or recreational activities you enjoy.

Nutrition

Good eating habits go hand-in-hand with fitness training. An athlete can be in good health without being physically fit, but he can't become physically fit without eating a well-balanced diet that contains protein, fats, and carbohydrates in the proper amounts. A healthy nutritional program for Americans was proposed years ago when the U.S. Department of Agriculture (USDA) and the Department of Health and Human Services (DHHS) published detailed guidelines for a good diet. The guidelines were issued in revised form in May 2000. These guidelines emphasized the importance of carbohydrates and the less important role of protein and fats in a healthful nutrition program.

Carbohydrates are sugars and starches that appear in two forms—either simple or complex. The simple form, found in processed foods like candy, soft drinks, or sweet desserts, is the one to avoid. These provide only "empty" calories—low quality nutrition—that may taste good momentarily but do nothing for overall health. It's not necessary to eliminate them entirely from your diet, but be selective. (Your dentist will be happy, too.) Sugar, in its natural form, is abundant in fresh fruit, and a better way to satisfy a sweet tooth is by eating a piece of fruit, rather than a candy bar.

Snacking in front of the television set seems to be another American dietary habit, but for the athlete who is serious about softball and getting fit, there is no place for high-fat, high-salt, high-calorie "junk food" in her diet. Try munching on an apple, tangerine, carrot or celery sticks while you watch your favorite show or when you need a snack during the day.

Complex carbohydrates are an athlete's best nutritional friend because they are his primary source of fuel. You'll find them in bread, vegetables of all colors (especially peas and beans), fruit, nuts, pasta, and whole grains (wheat, rice, corn, and oats.) They should make up about 60 percent of your daily food intake.

Protein is found in several foods—nuts, dairy products, and lean meats, poultry, and low-fat fish. A 16-ounce T-bone steak every day isn't needed to "build muscle." In fact, that's probably too much protein for your body to absorb efficiently; the rest just goes to waste. Try to keep your protein consumption to about 20 percent of what you eat each day, and you'll consume enough to build muscle, maintain it, and repair it when necessary.

Your body does need some fat, but not nearly as much as most Americans consume every day from a diet that is often overloaded with fat and salt. The fat you eat should come from margarine, vegetable oil, or nuts and should be no more than 20 percent of your daily intake of food. Fat has some benefits; it is an insulator in cold weather and an energy source, but a little goes a long way in keeping an athlete healthy and fit.

A Guide to Daily Food Choices

Fats, Oils, & Sweets
USE SPARINGLY

Milk, Yogurt, & Cheese Group
2-3 SERVINGS

Meat, Poultry, Fish, Dry
Beans, Eggs, & Nuts Group
2-3 SERVINGS

Vegetable Group
3-5 SERVINGS

Fruit Group
2-4 SERVINGS

**SERVING
KEY**
☐ - minimum serving
■ - above minimum
serving guidelines

Bread, Cereal, Rice, & Pasta Group
6-11 SERVINGS

Source: U.S. Department of Agriculture and the U.S.
Department of Health and Human Services

Don't skip meals—especially breakfast. Breakfast is like putting gas in your car—you need it to get started—and that meal should be a good, solid one–third of your daily calorie intake. Not hungry for breakfast in the morning? Try this once: Eat a light dinner the night before; you'll have an appetite in the morning, and that should help get you on a regular meal schedule. It is, perhaps, a cliché, but eating breakfast will make you feel better all day. Also, there is no nutritional law that requires a "traditional" breakfast. There is nothing wrong with eating a baked potato, having a hearty soup, or eating lean meat, fish, or poultry at your first meal of the day. The important point to learn is to eat well-balanced, nutritious meals throughout the day, starting with the first one.

A word on liquids: Avoid cola drinks, coffee, and tea. They are high in caffeine, which acts as a diuretic to take water from your body. The one liquid you should not avoid is water, which is 60 percent of your body's weight and needed to lubricate your joints and maintain your body's temperature. Water is also the transportation system for the nutrients you need to stay healthy, so don't neglect this crucial liquid. One to two quarts per day will keep your body well-lubricated and prevent dehydration.

The new dietary guidelines from the USDA and the DHHS suggest that Americans ". . . limit the intake of beverages and foods that are high in added sugars." For example, a Food and Drug Administration (FDA) study, published early in 2000, reported that soda consumption per person in the United States had reached 41 gallons in 1997. This is nearly double the 1970 consumption rate of 22 gallons. A 12-ounce can of soda contains 9 teaspoons of sugar, an amount that you could visualize by measuring this amount into a cup or glass. The sizes of soda containers have kept pace with consumption, from the standard 6.5-ounce bottle of the 1950s to today's 12-, 20-, and 64-ounce containers. As soda consumption has gone up, milk, juice, and water consumption has gone down. These high-calorie drinks don't contain the vitamins and minerals needed for good health, so limiting your consumption is probably a good idea.

A recent study at Harvard University of adolescent girls (whose bones are maturing) indicates that many are drinking more sodas, not eating calcium-rich foods, and not getting enough weight-bearing exercise, such as running or tennis. Long range, these dietary and exercise deficits can lead to thin, brittle bones that fracture easily.

The problem is of such concern that the DHHS, the Centers for Disease Control (CDC), and the National Osteoporosis Foundation are cooperating in an information campaign aimed at 9- to 12-year-old girls. The campaign will stress the importance of calcium in the diet, which foods are good sources of calcium, and the importance of combining weight-bearing exercise with calcium intake.

The guidelines also made statements about exercise and sodium (salt) in the diet. For the first time, Americans are urged to include "moderate daily exercise" of at least 30-minutes per day in their lifestyles and to ". . . choose and prepare foods with less salt." This means avoiding soy sauce, ketchup, mustard, pickles, and olives.

Finally, there are no "miracle foods" or "miracle diets" or "miracle pills" that will keep you in perfect health and physically fit. A well-balanced diet, paired with regular exercise, does not increase an athlete's reaction time. On the contrary, health, physical fitness, and a long life may become compromised.

Precautions

Approximately 40-50 million Americans smoke, and studies have shown that most of them began in their early teens. The use of cigarettes by teenagers is growing, and several steps are being proposed to limit sales to those younger than 18. The number of cigarettes smoked and the percentage of smokers have declined steadily over the last 15 years, but "social smoking"—those who smoke occasionally—is up. These social smokers have a sense that smoking is not harmful to health or an addiction, even though it is.

Based on recent statistical evidence from the Tobacco Intervention Network, young males seem most addicted to smokeless tobacco, wanting to imitate professional athletes, or succumbing to peer pressure.

Smokeless tobacco causes dental cavities—it is one-third sugar—and the irritation caused by holding a wad of tobacco in the mouth causes receding gums, gum disease, bone loss, and the inevitable tooth loss.

All drugs have side-effects, and smokeless tobacco is no different. It increases blood pressure and heart rate, and seems to increase the likelihood of kidney disease. Smokeless tobacco does not improve an athlete's reaction time. Both the National Institute of Drug Abuse and the American Psychological Association agree that smokeless tobacco can produce dependency and result in addiction.

The use of any tobacco product by officials is not strictly prohibited, but is certainly not recommended. Coaches, wrestlers, and team personnel at the high school level are considered guilty of unsportsmanlike conduct if they use tobacco products.

The Partnership for a Drug Free America believes that marijuana smoking among teens has reached epidemic proportions. Many youngsters think smoking marijuana is not dangerous and is a "safe" alternative to alcohol or tobacco. One reason for this misconception is that because there was less marijuana smoking in the 1980s, many young people have not seen "pothead burnout" among adults or their peers and are ignorant of the consequences.

The ramifications of smoking marijuana have not been publicized, but 30 years of research have pinpointed the effects: According to Monika Guttman, who writes extensively about drug use, "marijuana reduces coordination; slows reflexes; interferes with the ability to measure distance, speed and time; and disrupts concentration and short–term memory." (Everything on that list would be detrimental to any athlete, especially a softball player.)

Marijuana has six times as many carcinogens (cancer-causing agents) as tobacco. Today's marijuana is much more potent, creates dependency faster, and often becomes an "entrance" drug—one that can lead to dependence on "hard" drugs like cocaine.

Currently, nearly 12.5 million Americans use illegal drugs, and teenagers are the fastest-growing segment of first-time, illegal-drug users. Teens, especially, know that drugs are the most important problem they face—ahead of violence, sex issues, and getting into college. They need a clear message about dangerous, illegal, and unhealthy drugs.

Drug-prevention materials for young people and adults are available by calling the U.S. Department of Health and Human Services at this toll-free number: 1-800-729-6686.

Drugs of some type have been used by many athletes for many years. We don't expect this from Olympic competitors, but we know this is true. One reason given for taking drugs is to win medals. Perhaps that is why they have been misnamed "performance enhancing," when in reality they are not. Steroids, amphetamines, hormones, human growth hormone (hGH), and erythropoietin (EPO) are a few drugs specifically banned by the IOC.

Steroids (anabolic-androgenic steroids, or AAS) are another drug danger, with terrible consequences for the user. Steroid use by males can result in breast development, hair loss, acne, and yellow skin and eyes. Among females, breasts shrink, hair grows on the face and body, and menstrual cycles can become irregular. For both, the result of steroid use can be permanent stunting of body growth.

The food additive androstenedione, or "andro," has been identified as a steroid and is now illegal without medical reasons. On their own initiative, the IOC, the National Football League (NFL), the NCAA, and other sports organizations already have banned its use by athletes.

The psychological effects of steroid use are just as devastating, according to the American Sports Education Institute, which has noted the following: "Wide mood swings ranging from periods of violent, even homicidal, episodes known as 'roid rages' to depression, paranoid jealousy, extreme irritability, delusions, and impaired judgment."

The American Medical Association, the International Olympic Committee, the National Collegiate Athletic Association, and the National Football League have deplored the use of steroids for building muscle or improving athletic performance.

The negative impacts on an athlete's health of using EPO, for example, can range from sterility to the risk of heart attack, liver and kidney disease, and some cancers. These are permanent, not temporary, health problems. EPO has caused deaths in athletes, as have amphetamines, and no one knows yet the long-term effects on a normal-size person of using human growth hormone.

A partial list of the consequences of taking any of these drugs follows:

- *Creatine*: The side effects are dizziness, diarrhea, and cramps.

- *EPO*: It forces the heart to work harder, can cause heart attacks, strokes, and sudden death.

- *Anabolic steroids*: Higher cholesterol, "roid rages," perhaps liver disease and cancer, heart disease, brain tumors. Among women, hair on the face, lost hair from the head, acne, breast shrinkage, and cessation of menstrual periods.

- *Cyproterone Acetate*: Stops sexual development in women.

- *hGH*: The side effects are unusual bone growth (or acromegaly). The forehead, cheeks, jaw, hands, and feet grow grotesquely.

- *Amphetamines*: Temporary boosters that increase heart rate, blood pressure, and respiration. They do not boost performance levels; in fact, they actually decrease them.

The ASA has adopted a drug control policy that uses the same standards as the USOC. Any substance currently banned by the USOC and used by an athlete is considered "doping." The punishment for testing positive (and refusing to be tested is automatically considered positive) is:

- *First offense:* disqualification from all ASA competitions for a minimum of one year.

- *Second offense:* disqualification for two years minimum.

- *Third offense:* lifetime ban.

Vision and Dental Care

If you wear corrective lenses and want to play softball, talk to your eye doctor and ask him if contact lenses would be suitable for you. Today's contacts come in hard and soft materials, are lightweight, and some can be worn for hours at a time. In fact, there are disposable contact lenses that can be worn 24 hours a day, don't require special cleaning, and can be disposed of after seven days. The latter are fairly expensive, however, and may not be suitable for the young, growing athlete. Always check with your eye doctor and follow his recommendations for your unique needs. If you wear the traditional contacts, be sure to have your cleaning and wetting solutions with you at practices and games and let your coach know you wear contacts.

Wearing a mouth guard can prevent injury to your teeth, lips, cheeks, and gums, so wear it during practices and games. Concussions or other head and neck injuries can be minimized by wearing a properly fitted mouth guard made by your dentist. It is not bulky, will not restrict your breathing, fits snugly, and covers your front teeth so well that you'll hardly know you're wearing it.

No matter what sport you play, custom mouth guards can help to prevent oral injuries. They are especially important for young children just starting out in sports. In fact, getting used to wearing one early will make it easier to continue wearing one at the high school or college levels where competition is far more aggressive.

Physical Fitness

It's never too soon, or too late, to begin exercising and getting your body into good working order. If you are overweight, get winded easily, or are otherwise out of shape, you may have difficulty participating in softball games. Consult your physician, however, before beginning any fitness program and work only under the supervision of a qualified, knowledgeable coach or trainer.

Coaches can test the fitness of their players—either rookies or veterans—with a few simple exercises done in preseason. Then, there is time to work on improving fitness.

Strength and Balance

The player stands on one side of a bench and grasps the top with both hands. Then, while holding the top with both hands and keeping the feet together, the player jumps over the bench.

Hand Speed

Mark three spots on a smooth surface, e.g., a tabletop. Have the player keep one hand on the middle spot and use the other hand to tap the spots on either side. Alternate which hand remains on the center spot.

Strength
Have the player do sit-ups from a bent-knee position.

Balance
Have the player stand on one leg and raise the free leg so that it is straight and parallel to the floor.

Coordination and Agility
With the feet together, have the player jump over a line from side-to-side.

Flexibility
Have the player sit on the floor with his legs stretched out. Then, have him reach forward to touch his shins, ankles, toes, or the soles of his feet.

The Four Parts of Fitness
Physical fitness has four parts: muscle strength, muscle endurance, cardiovascular (heart, lungs, and blood vessels) endurance, and flexibility. Each part depends on the others to maintain physical fitness. Push-ups, for example, build strong muscles through muscle repetition. Muscle endurance

aims to work muscles over a period of time without tiring them. Sit-ups are great for this. Muscles need oxygen to function at peak levels, and this is why the heart, lungs, and blood vessels are so important to physical fitness. They sustain working muscles over long periods of time during practices and softball games.

Muscle Strength

Muscle strength can prevent aches and pains, keep the body aligned properly, and prevent injuries. Building this muscle strength requires fast and long exercise. The muscle gets "tired," but this is what builds strength. Muscles should feel a little uncomfortable but not painful. The goal is all-over muscle strength, since too much strength in one group of muscles can lead to an injury in another group. Strong muscles with low flexibility can lead to muscle pulls, while flexibility with low muscle strength can lead to dislocations.

Whether you use hand-held dumbbells or sophisticated exercise machines, strength-training techniques work the same way: they pit your muscles against resistance. (An athlete using equipment at a gym needs guidance from a fitness trainer.) Strength is built as resistance is increased, a concept called "progressive overload." Repeated stress thickens the fibers that make up muscles by increasing protein buildup. The thicker the muscle fibers, the stronger the muscles.

A strength-training session includes exercises for all the major muscle groups. This type of training is done in sets of 8 to 12 repetitions, using a weight just heavy enough so that only twelve repetitions can be produced.

Some suggested muscle strength exercises are abdominal curls, for a strong abdomen and lower back, and squats for strong shoulders, hips, lower back, buttocks, thighs, calves, and ankles. (A catcher or infielder might do 160-200 squats during a game.) Lifting two 3-pound weights, which can be books, quart bottles filled with water, or standard weights purchased at a sporting goods store, is good for building strength in arm muscles. (There are also ankle, body, and wrist weights.) Squeezing a hard rubber racquetball is one way to strengthen fingers and wrists and is convenient to do in spare moments. Take a day off in between workouts to give muscles recovery and muscle-building time.

Muscle Endurance

Muscle endurance exercises build stamina to play seven innings and help the body to perform at its best during a game under a variety of weather conditions: warm, cool, damp, hot and dry, or hot and humid.

This training repeats the same exercise many times, using a relatively light weight. Vigorous exercises such as jogging, bicycling, and swimming are excellent for achieving muscle endurance. They also increase heart and lung efficiency and improve an athlete's overall personal appearance. Muscle endurance training should be done only three times a week because muscle fibers tear slightly during exercise and need rest to rebuild themselves.

Cardiovascular Endurance

Cardiovascular endurance is achieved through exercises performed for at least 20 minutes. Walking, jogging, running, bicycling, swimming, dancing, and skipping rope are activities that raise the heart rate, take oxygen into the body, and move it to the muscles, which then provide the energy for the exercise being done. (Remember, a catcher needs to be able to run from home to first base in under three seconds.)

Weather and unhealthful air sometimes interfere with outdoor endurance exercises, so gyms have become more and more popular with athletes. Bowling is also good indoor exercise that can supplement a fitness program.

Stationary bicycles are widely available and can be "ridden" to fit a personal schedule that is not dependent on the weather.

Other indoor endurance exercises include jogging in place, jumping jacks, and doing side hops. When exercising on a rug, wear gym socks; on a hard floor, shoes that cushion the feet are best.

Flexibility

There are numerous flexibility exercises—bends, stretches, swings, twists, lifts, and raisers—which stretch out muscles that have "tightened" from vigorous exercise, as in a softball game or other competition. Muscle-pull injuries are common when flexibility is poor, even though muscle strength might be high. On the other hand, when flexibility is high, but muscle strength low, dislocations can occur.

Stretching and Warming Up

Regardless of your age, it's important that your body be flexible and relaxed. One of the best ways to maintain flexibility and relax muscles is to stretch every day, even on the days without practice or a game. Do not pull the body into exaggerated or painful positions—that is not stretching; that is torture. Such extremes are not helpful and may even cause an injury.

The point of stretching is to get the blood flowing and to "loosen" the muscles and tendons, which will help your flexibility and can reduce your chances of a pulled muscle or injury. Stretching exercises should start from the top, at the neck, and work down to the legs, with arm, shoulder, and lower-back exercises in between. Do each slowly and never stretch to a point that is painful. Motions should be fluid and the exercises done at a slow to medium pace, preferably in a warm environment. Follow a few simple guidelines for effective stretching and remember, also, to drink plenty of fluids, especially in warm weather. The body's lymph nodes need fluid to carry away impurities, and without fluid, the circulatory system cannot function effectively.

• Start with both feet on the ground, weight balanced

over the balls of the feet. Let arms hang loosely at sides. Wiggle fingers; then gently shake wrists. Next, shake arms. Rest.

- Raise arms and "reach for the sky." Roll up on the toes and stretch, reaching as high as possible with one hand. Hold this position for 10 seconds, then reach with the other hand and hold. Repeat this exercise five times.

- Rest hands on hips and, keeping the back straight and head forward, stretch to the left. Hold. Now arch the right arm over the head so that the fingers point to the left and down. Hold. (There should be a gentle stretch along the right side of the body.) Do the same exercise with the left arm, fingers pointing to the right and down. Hold. Repeat this exercise five times.

- Rest hands on hips and bend forward from the waist. Do not bounce. Stretch gently and hold. Tilt the chin down toward the chest, remove hands from hips, and let arms hang loosely. Wiggle fingers and shake arms. (There should be a gentle stretch along the backs of legs, up through the back and neck.) Return, slowly and smoothly without jerking, to a standing position and rest.

To stretch legs, move to an area where there is something sturdy to hang onto and ample room to swing the legs freely.

- Stand with feet about 8 to 9 inches apart. Upper torso should be balanced over the hips, head up (but not tilted back), and the eyes looking forward. Body should be straight, but not stiff. If right-handed, shift the weight to the left leg and begin the exercise with the right leg. If left-handed, reverse the order. Hold onto a chair or other support with the left hand and gently swing the right leg forward and backward 15 times. Turn around. Do the exercise 15 times swinging the opposite leg. Rest.

- Hold onto a support structure and balance the weight over the left leg. Stick the right leg out in front, toes up toward the sky, heel no more than 6 inches off the ground. Now, with the back straight but not stiff, push the right heel forward—not down toward the ground, but forward. The calf muscle should stretch. Do not bounce. Hold for a count of 10 seconds, return heel and toes to starting position, and lower the right leg to the ground. Balance the weight equally over both feet and rest. Turn around and repeat the exercise with the opposite leg.

After completing a set of stretching exercises, keep your body warm.

Motor Fitness
Motor fitness includes coordination, speed, balance, and agility. Body muscles and body senses, especially the eyes, build coordination. Repeating certain eye and body movements—catching a ball, for example—builds coordination. Speed is built through brief exercises that demand energy and effort. Short sprints are excellent speed builders.

Conditioning Programs
Many softball players play volleyball, basketball, and racquetball to stay in shape and keep their stamina level high in the off-season. They might follow a program of jogging, running, and working out at a gym. Year-round conditioning is advocated by some coaches who prepare their athletes by dividing the year into phases or periods, with different goals and objectives for each period. Phase One, for example, might begin 6 to 12 weeks before the opening of softball season with emphasis on flexibility exercises, aerobics, and muscle strength and muscle endurance exercises. Coaches of beginners up to Olympic competitors stress fitness because

they know that athletes who stay fit are less likely to sustain injuries, and recover faster when they are injured.

College coaches expect several hours per day of fitness training at this level, with emphasis placed on strength, endurance, speed, and sport-specific exercises. Practicing softball techniques is excellent exercise while, at the same time, it is helping the athletes to perfect their skills. Three sport-specific exercises that a coach might consider are "feeding," fielding ground balls, and running the bases. These are especially helpful at the beginning level when a coach is trying to teach youngsters and to develop a team all at the same time.

- All players line up in pairs about 6 feet apart. The first pair starts off at a jog and while jogging, the players toss a ball back and forth without slowing, stopping, or dropping the ball. Infielders, especially, should benefit from this drill, but it's good practice for the entire team.

- Two infielders face each other while in the semi-crouch position, i.e., knees and hips flexed and the weight on the balls of the feet. Staying 5 feet apart and remaining in the semi-crouch position, one player rolls a ball to the left of the other player, who fields the ball and throws (tosses) it back. Then, the first player repeats the roll to the right of the second player. The exercise changes, with the second player rolling the ball to the right and then to the left of the first player. During the entire exercise, both players remain in the semi-crouch position.

- Place a marker of some type—highway cones work— before first and third bases and tell players they will turn left when they reach these. Then, have players line up single file and one after another, jog to first base, sprint to second base, jog to third base, and sprint home.

Reconditioning

As important as a conditioning program is the reconditioning program that takes place after an athlete has suffered an injury. Athletes want to play, but the decision to return to the lineup should be made by the player's parents, family physician, and the coach, all working together.

A sprained ankle, for example, might be rehabilitated with easy jogs at first; the player would gradually build up to running. Ice can be used to reduce any swelling that might occur, and/or an elastic bandage might be worn.

Everyone involved should be patient and not allow the player to return to play until the injury is no longer a problem. Semi-recovered players hurt themselves as much as their team.

Note: This book is in no way intended to be a substitute for the medical advice of a personal physician. We advise and encourage the reader to consult with his/her physician before beginning this or any other weight management, exercise, or fitness program. The authors and the publisher disclaim any liability or loss, personal or otherwise, resulting from the suggestions in this book.

7

Safety and First Aid

Softball is one of the safer sports for youngsters and young adults, but learning a few common safety rules can prevent serious injury, especially from collisions in the infield or outfield. Since all athletes get bumps and bruises, and occasionally more serious injuries, there are a few precautions to take at practices or play.

Safety First

Many collisions happen, but just as many can be avoided.

- Know where the ball is at all times. This rule applies to players on the bench as well as those in the field.

- Teach fielders to talk to one another, saying "I've got it," or "Yours," or some other appropriate verbal signal.

- Teach infielders, especially, to move inside the diamond to avoid collisions with base runners.

For practices and games, there are safety precautions that can prevent needless injuries.

- Stow equipment in one area. Players should keep their bats in this area when not in use.

- Always wear a helmet to practices and games. It's designed to protect your head and ears from injury.

- If your dentist has recommended a mouth guard, be sure to have it in your mouth during practices and games.

- Wear the right clothes for practice sessions—probably your team uniform.

- Players with long hair should wear headbands or other ornamentation to keep their hair under control so it is not a hindrance or distraction.

- Leave jewelry—watches, rings, earrings, etc.— in a locker or duffel bag.

- Go through a warm-up session and do stretching exercises before the actual practice or game begins. This prevents muscle strains and other aches and pains. Muscle strains are fairly common injuries for softball players, but their incidence can be reduced through a preseason conditioning program and warming up before a game or practice.

- Skip a practice or two when you're not feeling well. Recovery will be quicker than if you had practiced or competed while "under the weather."

- Drink plenty of water. Dehydration can occur quickly; don't wait until you're thirsty to get a drink. Some coaches recommend sports drinks and think they are useful, but water tastes just as good and is usually free, with no cans or bottles to dispose of.

A pre-practice and pregame safety check might include the following:

- Conducting a thorough check of the field and any structures to be used. Are the bases fastened securely? Are there objects (rocks, glass, trash) that can trip a player or cause an injury?

- Determining that all the players have equipment that fits properly, not being too small or too large.

- Determining that all the players understand how to practice safely and not get in the way of other practicing players.

- Determining that all the players have basic skills, know the rules, and understand signals from the coaches.

The First Aid Kit

In all sports, someone sustains an injury of some kind. It's wise to know what to do to handle those inevitable bumps, bruises, scrapes, or more serious injuries. Having a well-stocked first aid kit handy is recommended. It should include the following:

- Adhesive tape in different sizes

- Adhesive bandages in different shapes and sizes

- Ammonia caps for dizziness

- Antiseptic solution for minor scrapes

- Antiseptic soap for washing a wound area

- Aspirin, or its equivalent, for simple headaches. For youth teams, no medication should be given without written, parental permission, signed and dated, authorizing the disbursement of aspirin, or any other medicine.

- Blanket to cover an injured player, since warmth reduces the chance of shock

- Cold packs

- Elastic wraps of various sizes

- Eyewash solution

- Gauze pads

- Hank's solution (trade name, Save-A-Tooth®) for a knocked-out tooth

- Plastic bottle filled with fresh water

- Sterile cotton sheets that can be cut to fit

- Scissors and, perhaps, an eyedropper and tweezers

- Tissues and premoistened towelettes

- Disposable towels

It is a good idea to have a list of emergency telephone numbers taped inside the first aid kit, but in a real emergency, dial 911. Know the location of a telephone and have some spare change handy in the first aid kit. A physician, nurse, or other trained health care professional will often be part of the staff at softball games, and can take care of serious injuries when they occur. But, never assume that precautions have been taken. Check in advance to be sure; be prepared.

Coaches may find these guidelines helpful:

- *Always remain calm.* Don't panic or appear flustered. Others will take their behavior cues from you.

- *Don't try to be a doctor.* When in doubt about the severity of any injury, send the player to a doctor or let the doctor, nurse, or health-care professional on duty at the game make the decision.

- *Never move a player who may have a serious injury.* Don't try to move a player off the field or into the locker room. This can make a serious injury worse. Be safe, not sorry, and call in the designated professionals if you have doubts about any injury. Under no circumstances should an unconscious player be moved! Stay with him until the professionals arrive.

Treatment
To treat common injuries, the following guidelines are suggested:

Scrapes and Burns

Wash mild scrapes and burns with an antiseptic cleaning solution and cover with sterile gauze. This is usually all that is needed to promote quick healing of these injuries.

Muscle Pulls, Sprains, Strains, and Bruises

Rest, Ice, Compression, and Elevation (**RICE**) are the steps needed to handle these injuries and about all that is needed in the way of treatment. Have the player stop and rest, apply ice, compress with an elastic bandage, and elevate the injured arm, leg, knee, or ankle. Ice reduces swelling and pain, and should be left on the injured area until it feels uncomfortable. Remove the ice pack and rest for 15 minutes, then reapply. These are the immediate steps to take until the doctor arrives. **RICE** reduces the swelling of most injuries and speeds up recovery. Over the next few days, the injury should be treated with two to three 20-minute sessions per day at two-and-one-half hour intervals. This should provide noticeable improvement. Don't overdo the icing; 20 minutes is long enough. In most cases, after two or three days, or when the swelling has stopped, heat can be applied in the form of warm-water soaks. Fifteen minutes of warm soaking, along with a gradual return to motion, will speed the healing process right along. Seek the advice of a sports-medicine professional prior to starting a treatment plan. Specially shaped pads are useful for knee and ankle injuries, and they can be used in combination with ice, compression, and elevation. For a simple bruise apply an ice pack.

Another approach to use after two or three days, and if your doctor agrees, is to begin Motion, Strength, and Alternative (**MSA**) exercise. The American Institute for Preventive Medicine recommends:

- *Motion*: Moving the injured area and reestablishing its range of motion.

- *Strength*: Working to increase the strength of the injured area once any inflammation subsides and your range of motion starts to return.

- *Alternative*: Doing regularly an alternative exercise that does not stress the injury.

Cuts and Other Wounds

Spikes and cleats can cause deep cuts, which should be cleaned and covered, with the player sent to a physician who can determine the need for stitches or a tetanus shot.

Fractures and Broken Bones

Small cuts need pressure to slow down bleeding. Then, wash with an antiseptic solution, cover with sterile gauze taped in place, and apply pressure. Of course, any deep or large cut might need stitches, and the player should see a doctor as soon as possible.

Head, Hand, and Foot Injuries

Blows to the upper part of the head, especially near the eyes, can cause bleeding under the skin; the result is a black eye or eyes. An ice pack applied to the area will keep down the swelling until a doctor can look at the injury.

Normally, the eye washes out most foreign particles by its ability to produce tears, but if this doesn't work, use eye cleaning solution to wash out the irritant. A few simple guidelines to follow are:

- Don't rub the eye or use anything dirty, like a cloth or finger, to remove the irritant.

- With clean hands, pull the eyelid forward and down, while looking down at the floor.

- Flush with eyewash, or use a clean, sterile cloth, to remove any particle visible and floating on the eye.

If the foreign object remains, tape a clean gauze pad over the eye and have the player see a doctor.

Nosebleeds usually don't last very long. Have the player sit quietly and apply a cold pack, while pinching the bleeding nostril at its base.

A knocked-out tooth can be successfully replanted if it is stored and transported properly. The tooth should be placed in a transport container containing a solution such as Hank's or Viaspan®, which is available over-the-counter at a drug store.

The coach and all medical personnel at a softball game should be alert to the importance of how to care for a knocked-out tooth. With immediate and proper attention to storage and transport, an injured player may be able to have a knocked-out tooth replanted successfully.

Jammed and/or broken fingers can be hard to distinguish. Use a cold pack to control swelling and pain, but if there is no improvement within an hour, send the player for an X-ray. A dislocated finger should be elevated and immobilized. Use a sling for a dislocated shoulder. The player should then receive medical attention from a professional.

Do not move a seriously injured player, but get prompt medical attention or call for emergency aid. If there is a wait for assistance, cover the injured player with a lightweight blanket, since warmth will reduce the chance of shock. Any player who has a broken bone should be seen by a doctor.

To safely move a person with an arm, wrist, hand, or leg injury, follow these steps:

- A finger with mild swelling can be taped gently to an adjacent finger.

- An elastic bandage may be wrapped gently around an injured wrist to support the wrist. Do not wrap heavily and do not pull the bandage tight.

- If the player has a possible broken leg or arm, the best approach is not to move the leg or arm in any manner. A cold pack can be used to lessen discomfort until medical personnel arrive, and the player should be kept warm with a blanket or covering to avoid shock.

Fractures and broken bones should be treated the same whether the bone is cracked, chipped, or broken. A fracture can be recognized by some or all of the following conditions:

- A part of the body is bent or twisted from its normal shape

- A bone has pierced the skin

- Swelling is severe and more than the swelling associated with a typical sprain or bruise

- A hand or foot becomes extremely cold, which may indicate pinching of a major blood vessel

Youngsters heal faster than adults, so it's important to get them prompt medical attention when a fracture occurs.

Blisters

The best "medicine" for blisters is prevention. Well-fitting softball shoes and socks can go a long way toward preventing this annoying, painful injury. Any blisters that do occur should be kept clean and covered with a bandage, especially if the blister breaks. Over-the-counter medications to treat blisters are available, but follow the advice of a trainer or doctor on these.

Breathing and Heat Problems

Getting the wind "knocked out of you" might happen during a game. Not much can be done to treat this, but breathing will return to normal more quickly if you can relax and take easy breaths.

Heat stroke and heat exhaustion do occur, but they can be minimized or avoided if players take plenty of water breaks. Coaches should monitor their players during practices and games to be sure the youngsters aren't getting dehydrated. If heat stroke or exhaustion do occur, have the player lie down where it's cool and call an ambulance.

By following the guidelines in this chapter, the extent and severity of injuries can be reduced and treatment minimized so that the player can return to the team and game confidently. Knowing what to do is beneficial to players, coaches, and parents in and out of the sport.

Blood Rule

The following is from *The 1998 Official Rules of Softball* published by the Amateur Softball Association of America:

> A player, coach, or umpire who is bleeding or who has blood on his uniform shall be prohibited from participating further in the game until appropriate treatment can be administered. If medical care or treatment is administered in a reasonable length of time, the individual will not have to leave the game. The length of time that is considered reasonable is left to the umpire's judgment. Uniform rule violations will not be enforced if a uniform change is required. The umpire shall:
>
> A. Stop the game and immediately call a coach, trainer, or other authorized person to the injured player and allow treatment.
>
> B. Apply the rules of the game regarding substitution, short-handed player and re-entry if necessary.

8

Organizing a Softball Team

Just as parents are the first "real life" role models for children, teachers and coaches come next. Coaches have immediate and quite visible responsibilities for their charges and need all the assistance and assistants they can find.

Coaches

While the obligations of coaches are broad and deep and extend beyond practices and competitions to include other members of the community, there is genuine satisfaction to be gained from helping youngsters in their personal and physical development. Building character, integrity, and respect, and assuring the physical well-being of players are integral parts of coaching duties and should be included in the total learning experience of young softball players. Therefore, set the example you want them to follow—match words and deeds. Be on time for practices, keep yourself fit and healthy, praise and criticize positively. Know the rules, including the expected conduct of players and coaches. Kids develop an intuitive alarm that goes off (loudly) when someone breaks the rules. They are also quick to pick up on body language and the tone of a coach's voice. Be fair, and never use your position of authority to gain an unfair advantage for yourself or your ballplayers.

A parent, if coaching his own child on a team, has a situation that is different from the usual parent-child relationship. For example, how should the child address the parent at softball practice and during a game? As a coach, will you expect more (or less) from your child than from other children? Both parent and child need to talk about and understand their different roles in advance.

Besides being a teacher and having a good grounding in the sport, a sense of humor, perspective, and diplomatic skills are invaluable. A coach knows that winning is not everything and that sometimes a team should win but doesn't due to circumstances beyond its control—the weather, a bad day for the team, or the other team was better that day. Never assign blame; no one loses deliberately. Don't take a loss personally.

ASA's VIP group for coaches can help you become a better coach, even if you have years of experience. The ASA offers coaching schools, clinics, and materials, including videos, that provide visual help on different parts of the game, especially important when a coach has a limited amount of time and few assistants. Don't be afraid to ask for help from players, former coaches, or current coaches. A first-year coach may want to watch as many softball games as possible in order to learn the game.

Organization
If you and other volunteers are organizing a softball team, several steps are involved. A few include creating publicity to locate potential players, finding a practice field, conducting tryouts, holding practice sessions, and playing softball games.

Publicity
To locate players and spread the word that a team is being organized, put posters in local retail stores, notices in company newsletters, information on high school bulletin boards, and publicity in local newspapers. Talk to friends who play softball

and spread the news by word of mouth. Tuck flyers under car windshield wipers at the local mall or on doorknobs. *Caution: Never put literature or flyers in anyone's mailbox. That is against the law.*

ASA/USA Softball

Photo finish. Men's slow pitch

Flyers could announce when the first tryouts will be (if a practice field has been reserved) and where, when, and at what time. Provide phone numbers or e-mail addresses to contact for more information, and state whether players should bring their own equipment.

Playing or Practice Field

The coach or an assistant should locate a practice field and learn when it is available. A field with high usage that serves a variety of softball teams probably has a schedule that will indicate when it's available. Have several dates and times in mind to ensure getting a date and time that are open. Check in advance whether there is a fee and how it is to be paid.

ASA/USA Softball

The third out. Mens' fast pitch

Tryouts

Preparing and organizing paperwork are necessary steps before the tryout session. Compile information sheets on yourself and your assistants, including names and contact numbers. Have practice and game schedules ready, along with uniform requirements and the appropriate rules and regulations. If the team will be playing in a league, there may be league forms to distribute and complete. Each player should receive a sign-up sheet and list his name, address, contact number, age, and the position he wants to play. In addition, coaches and their assistants should familiarize themselves with the Americans with Disabilities Act (ADA) and the ASA rules that apply to slow pitch softball.

Later, after the team is formed, the team should have player insurance, and as a safety measure, medical forms and parental consent forms, especially if the players are not yet adults. Coaches have legal responsibilities and must warn parents and players of the risks involved. Therefore, maintaining accurate records is vital.

Once all the potential players are assembled, introduce yourself and your assistants, giving a brief overview of what you expect the team to be. Provide information on the league the team will compete in (if that is the case), how often practices will be held, and how often the team will compete in softball games. If some games will be played away from home, the amount of travel time should be estimated and that information provided.

To get a general idea of players' fitness, have them do a general warm-up first of jogging and stretching. (See Chapter 6, "Health and Fitness," for other suggested fitness tests.) Then have players divide into three groups by position played— infielders, outfielders, and pitchers and catchers.

Once the players have been divided, get player information sheets filled out and make name tags for each player. Follow this with skill drills to assess ability.

Have players play catch with a partner and practice throwing and catching ground balls and fly balls. Have pitchers take turns pitching batting practice. Have a few players at a time run the bases, or individually run from home to first. The coach or an assistant may want to time these runs.

Outfielders should get practice catching fly balls; infielders fielding ground balls. Pitchers need to demonstrate their speed and accuracy.

ASA/USA Softball

Try to steal on me, I dare you! Girls' fast pitch

The coach and his assistants should each have a clipboard with the names and positions played of the players trying out, with room to note comments on skills, potential, and overall condition.

End the tryout with information on when the team members will be selected and when they'll be notified. Announce the when, where, and time of the next practice and remind players to complete any forms and return them.

Practices

Organization is the key to successful practices. Always include a 5- to 10-minute warm-up session, stretching exercises, and a 5- to 10-minute cool-down after practice. The warm-up exercises are not as strenuous as those done in a regular conditioning program, but they should decrease soreness later on and minor injuries, such as tears and strains. (See Chapter 6, "Health and Fitness," for suggested stretching exercises.) Weather conditions on any particular day will help the coach to determine the length and demands of practice. Players might take turns leading the session and gain some valuable leadership skills while working with the team.

Once players are warmed up, have them work on the fundamentals: throwing, catching, batting, and base running. Follow this by fielding and catching drills—handling ground balls, and catching fly balls and pop-ups. Next, practice executing double plays, covering bases, and backing up a base. Some refinements—stealing a base, how to slide—might be included as the team coalesces.

If a team is at the beginning level, players probably will have to be taught all the basics: batting, hitting, catching (thrown and batted balls), fielding, and running the bases. This is when good teaching skills are essential.

Use simple language that is brief and to the point. Short attention spans can be overcome by telling and showing, showing and telling. Have players repeat and demonstrate. Discipline players only when they are taking dangerous risks or simply "fooling around" and not paying attention, but don't discipline anyone for an honest mistake. Smile frequently.

Games

Several pregame preparations are done by the home team:

- The playing field has to be available for a certain date and time and the visiting team notified. A map and directions may be provided for them.

- A permit (if needed) must be secured and paid for if there is a charge.

- The field needs to be laid out and the bases secured.

- If there is an admission charge, or a donation requested, someone needs to be designated to handle that responsibility.

- If there are lights and a public address system, someone needs to know how to check and operate those systems.

- An umpire has to be hired. If there is a fee involved for his service, who pays?

- There should be a designated scorekeeper.

- The home team customarily provides the softballs, but players provide their own gear.

- Do a pregame check of the playing field for safety.

- Finally, play the game and have fun.

Umpires

Umpires have responsibilities that are as important to softball games as those of coaches, players, and fans. They know the rules, signals, and procedures and understand their purpose. Umpires control the game by displaying their self-confidence, by exhibiting their knowledge of the game, and by making calls promptly. They are courteous, of course, but not too friendly because that could be misinterpreted as favoritism toward one team.

Being an umpire can be a lonely job. The umpire has no friends during a game (except for the other members of his crew), especially when making difficult calls. Patience, good judgment, and courtesy are prerequisites for the position. When any of his decisions are questioned—and surely some will be—an umpire must be prepared to explain his decision in a calm, but firm, manner.

Umpires need to be as physically fit and healthy as the players and coaches. They should follow a conditioning program before the season begins because it is especially important to strengthen the legs and back before the first ballgame. During the season, weight control and fluids replacement are the two areas of major concern for them.

Umpires need the mental attitude and emotional stability to handle the many "ups and downs" of umpiring. And, certainly, it is far more important to be a part of the game because you love it. Any desire for extra income should be secondary.

Judgment
This skill is learned through the experience of umpiring games. Good judgment is acquired by facing difficult situations on the field and resolving them with a display of firmness and self-control. Judgment means an umpire's temper must be controlled so he can control the game. That earns the respect of all concerned.

Mechanics and Technique
The mechanics of umpiring cover the who, what, where, and sometimes why of the game. Knowing well these four "w's" separates the professional umpire from the amateur. Included in mechanics are your position for a play and how to cover it. The correct position for a play must be learned, then the coverage practiced in order to get a "feel" for it. It is crucial that an umpire not get in the way of players or the ball, so position and coverage are always important.

An umpire's technique is his style and how he behaves. Obviously, each umpire is different, but one thing umpires should all have in common is hustle. Players hustle off the field between innings. Umpires should be just as ready to assume their positions by setting a good example for everyone. This keeps the game moving and avoids distractions that can add unnecessary minutes to a game.

How to Gain Respect

There are several elements involved on the way to gaining the status of a respected umpire.

- Stay fit. The athletes do, and umpires must keep pace with them.

- Be neat, clean, and well-groomed for your duties.

- Make calls promptly, but not hastily. Be sure the play is complete. Use a firm voice so everyone understands you are in charge.

- Communicate with your partner(s) and support their decisions during a game. Don't interfere; wait until you are asked for help or assistance.

- Know the rules. Some of your decisions will become routine and will be made almost automatically. Regular study of the rules and the use of visualization techniques will make real game situations easier to call and to rule on. Never guess; everyone will know it.

- Ignore the spectators. Pretend you are deaf and develop a thick skin.

- Don't be a showboat or an actor. This is not a performance; you are not a star.

- Be professional, courteous, and businesslike.

- Finally, to err is human. You will misjudge plays. Go on to the next and do your best.

Ethics for Umpires

All professions have ethical guidelines. Ethics rules for umpires include the following:

- Honor your contracts.

- Watch other umpires, learn from them, and study the rules.

- Focus on the game and players.

- Look like an umpire in dress and appearance.

- Be fair. Show no favoritism.

- Cooperate with your fellow umpires.

- Be firm, positive, and dignified.

- Be ready to take charge of the game.

- Do not smoke or drink alcoholic beverages anywhere near the game. In the case of alcohol, never drink any before a game.

- Keep team information confidential.

- Remember that the game is more important than any of its parts—players, coaches, or umpires.

9

Guidelines

For everyone involved to enjoy a softball game, good sportsmanship must extend beyond the field of play and include parents and spectators, as well as players and coaches.

Parents

Softball is meant to be fun for everyone involved, and parents need to be supportive and enthused about the sport, and keep it all in perspective by focusing on achievements, rather than miscues. Those attitudes will build the confidence a youngster needs to succeed, not just in softball, but in other activities as well. Parents are the earliest role models for children; consequently, children carry over into sports the attitudes they have learned from their parents.

Parents want their kids to excel, to come out on top, and to be winners. Basking in their glory—even though it's reflected—is a powerful emotion. Softball is a team sport, and there will be one team that finishes the game with fewer runs than the other. Parents need to be prepared to handle defeat in an adult manner by praising the effort involved and avoiding a litany of "What you (or the team or the coach) should have done was . . ." Most youngsters are usually well aware of their skills, and they don't need to be told or made to feel somehow deficient when their team loses. Along with that caution, parents should recognize the achievement of the winning team and never criticize the officials or coaches. Coaches and officials are usually volunteers and are probably parents who have children involved in the sport. They have the same emotions as parents—in fact, their feelings may be even more intense, since they are more directly involved. They have to be objective, treat all players with the same respect and regard, and follow the rules. Non-coaching parents have similar obligations.

Children benefit from participating in softball, and the confidence gained carries over to other parts of growing up: working with others, developing self-discipline, learning good health habits, and acquiring self-esteem.

There are not just physical benefits involved, but psychological as well. Athletes seem to have better mental health by having a positive channel for their youthful energy. A recent finding of the President's Council on Physical Fitness and Sports stated that athletics promote health in adulthood, and reduce stress and depression. Furthermore, athletes stay in school and seem more motivated to continue their education by attending college.

Young girls, especially, need encouragement to participate in sports, which for years have been promoted as "male only" activities. Stereotypes abound about athletics not being "feminine," and many young women "tune out" sports because of these negative stereotypes.

Parents can help daughters to overcome these stereotypes by demonstrating an interest in sports, especially any that interest their children. However, a parent's favorite sport may not interest a child. Don't push; do encourage.

Before a child becomes involved in a particular sport, parents should decide whether or not he or she is physically and psychologically ready for a competitive sport. A preseason physical from the family physician is a first step in determining whether a youngster is healthy and would benefit from participation. The child is still growing, so parents, the coach, and assistants should recognize and make allowances for this. (Ideally, children play with other children of nearly the same *size,* not necessarily the same age.)

ASA/USA Softball/International Softball Federation

The fans were in unison at softball's Olympic debut
...USA! USA! USA!

Don't hesitate to inquire about the coach's qualifications and experience. Training in batting, throwing, running, and all phases of the game should be given by someone who is knowledgeable and trained in the proper methods. Incorrect training can cause nagging injuries that decrease the enjoyment of the game for everyone. Pitchers, especially, practice for hours and must be coached properly so that arm, elbow, and wrist are not injured by repetitive stress.

Enthusiasm for the sport may drop off after a few practices or games. A parent should try to be fairly certain of the child's commitment and ability to work and play easily with other youngsters before signing that child up for softball.

Recent studies of young athletes indicate that the quality of their play improves when parents attend games. In addition to a youngster's commitment, his parents should also make one.

ASA/USA Softball/International Softball Federation

Softball packed them in at the 1996 Olympic Summer Games

Fans

Before attending a softball game, learn a few basics about the sport, and your enjoyment will increase along with your understanding. Observe a few common courtesies—stay seated, don't block anyone's view, don't shout at officials, don't criticize players or argue with other spectators—and you'll be welcome at every game.

Volunteers

Being a volunteer requires some extra time and a desire to make a difference in the lives of young people. Softball is a golden opportunity for everyone in a family or the community-at-large to get involved and make this difference. Today more than ever, young people need to know adults care about them and their futures, since they are bombarded every day by enticements to use drugs, join gangs, or engage in other activities that promote a dangerous lifestyle.

There are many ways to help your local softball team, as a coach or leader, official or fan. When a local team is sponsoring a tournament, there are a number of ways to help. For league games or a tournament, volunteer to:

- Staff the on-site registration table

- Be the scorekeeper

- Be the announcer

- Prepare forms, information sheets, and maps

- Be the tournament coordinator

- Head the cleanup committee

- Coordinate the volunteers

- Be the equipment manager

- Be the team's treasurer

- Be the team's photographer

- Videotape practices and individual players for the coaches

- Arrange transportation for "away" games

Teams and Players

Learning to be a member of a team is one of life's important skills. Working together, within a set of rules, toward a goal rewards everyone involved with a sense of accomplishment and pride in the effort. Win or lose, everyone learns from the experience. Sometimes limits are placed on individual desires in order to further the goals of the group. No one always gets exactly what he wants; quite often compromise is necessary. Mutual aid and dependability are required from all members of a team. Be supportive of your teammates and let them know you can be depended upon to show up for practices and games.

There are specific things you can do for yourself and your team:

- Support each player
- Offer encouragement, especially in defeat, and congratulations in victory
- Learn how to win and how to lose—graciously
- Be positive and compliment good playing skills
- Let the coaches correct errors—that's their job
- Don't be a showoff
- Go to every practice, do your best, and show that you are trying
- Don't dwell on "mistakes"—yours or anyone else's
- Errors and mistakes are not the end of the world—that's how life is
- Never be guilty of taunting
- Set a good example by staying healthy and physically fit

As a softball player, keep the sport in perspective and fit it into your entire life. That means learn to assign priorities. You'll have to stay fit and healthy and get enough sleep each night. Many schools require that a certain level of academic achievement—otherwise known as good grades—be maintained in order to participate in sports. Thus, school attendance and schoolwork cannot be neglected in favor of concentrating on athletics. Playing softball should be fun and rewarding.

The following suggestions may help to increase both the fun and the rewards:

- Play because you want to; don't let anyone "pressure" you into playing

- Obey the rules

- Don't argue, whine, or gripe about calls or decisions

- Keep your temper in hand and never retaliate

- Prepare, do your best, and have fun

- Finally, the Golden Rule does work—treat everyone the way you want to be treated

ASA/USA Softball/Doug Hoke

Olympic gold medalist Leah O'Brien-Amico and her fans at Superball, a pre-Olympic event

Being a dependable member of your team, learning from your coaches, following their guidelines, and playing fair with opponents can make your softball experience a lifelong guide to achieving other goals.

Players should behave in such a way that they are a credit to their parents, communities, schools, the sport, and themselves. The image of softball depends on your behavior and appearance, not only at games, but also while traveling, and at school or away. Your conduct can influence your teammates, whether you win or lose.

10

Glossary

AAU Amateur Athletic Union.

ASA Amateur Softball Association. The National Governing Body (NGB) for softball in the United States and the representative of the sport on the USOC.

Base on Balls Occurs when a pitcher throws four balls outside the strike zone to a batter.

Base Path The line that runs between home plate and each base. It varies in length, depending on which type of softball game is played.

Batter's Box Area on the left and right sides of home plate where the hitter stands when it is his turn at bat.

Batting Order The official order in which players will bat.

Blood Rule Rule adopted by the ASA that describes the procedure for handling any blood on players or clothing during a game.

Catch A catch occurs whenever a ball is caught in the glove, hand, or both.

Catcher's Box The area behind home plate where the catcher crouches.

Coach's Box Area by first and third bases where coaches stand.

Count The balls and strikes on a batter, *e.g.*, three balls and two strikes.

Defensive Team The softball team in the field; the team not batting.

Double A hit by an offensive player that allows him to advance to second base.

Double Play A defensive play that results in two base runners being called out on one batted ball.

Down The number of outs in an inning.

Dugout The area where the team, coaches, and equipment remain when not on defense or at bat.

ERA Earned run average.

Error A mistake made by a player during a game that benefits the other team.

Extra-base hit A hit that allows a batter to advance safely beyond first base.

Fair Ball Any ball hit on the ground or in the air within the two foul lines.

Fast Pitch Softball Olympic-style softball played with nine players. The ball is thrown underhand, but with less arc than in slow pitch.

Fly Ball Any ball hit to the outfield.

Force-out   The play that results when a fielder has the ball and is at a base that a hitter is running to. First-base force-outs are a common example.

Foul Ball   Any ball hit outside the foul lines.

Foul Tip   A ball hit directly to the catcher's glove or hand and not higher than the batter's head, which is caught by the catcher.

Grip   A 10- to 15-inch section of every bat just above the knob. Also the way in which a hitter grips a bat.

Home Run   A hit that no outfielder can field. Hitter advances around the bases and crosses home plate.

Home Team   The team that plays regularly on one field. The home team bats second, at the "bottom" of an inning.

Infield   The diamond area of a softball field.

Infield Fly   A fly ball caught by an infielder.

Infielder   A player whose responsibilities are on the diamond area of the field.

Inning   One complete turn at bat for each team, which is the result of three outs for each team.

IOC   International Olympic Committee. The governing body for all sports included in the Olympic Games.

ISF   International Softball Federation. The international governing body for softball.

JOP   Junior Olympic Player. The name for the ASA's youth program.

Lead-off Batter	The first batter up in either half of each inning.
Line Drive	A ball hit hard, low, and fast; usually is difficult to field.
Modified Pitch	The game that combines parts of fast pitch and slow pitch softball.
MSA	Acronym for Motion, Strength, Alternative Exercise. An approach to handling an injury.
NCAA	National Collegiate Athletic Association.
Offensive Team	The team at bat in any inning.
On-deck Batter	The batter who is waiting to bat next.
Outfield	The area of the softball field covered by the left, center, and right fielders.
Pitcher's Plate	A 24-inch long by 6-inch wide wood or rubber slab. The pitcher begins pitching from the pitcher's plate.
Pivot Foot	In fast pitch, the pitcher's foot that stays in contact with the plate before pushing off. In slow pitch, the pitcher's foot that stays in contact with the plate until the ball is released.
Pop-up	A ball hit high and up in the air and usually caught by an infielder.
Presenting the Ball	The pitcher's body, feet, and hand positions just before pitching.
RBI	Run(s) batted in.
RICE	Rest, Ice, Compression, and Elevation.
Runner	Any player on base.

Scorecard	Card that lists the batting order of players and their positions. Used to record the softball game as it is played.
Scoring Position	Positions on base—usually second and third base—where players are in position to score on a base hit.
Shutout	Preventing the opposing team from scoring a run.
Single	A hit that allows a batter to reach first base.
Sixteen-inch	Softball played with a sixteen-inch ball and on a field with shorter minimum distances to the outfield, between bases, and from the pitcher to home plate.
Slow Pitch	Most-played form of the game. Teams have ten players, and the pitcher throws the ball in a high arc. Often, such games are high-scoring.
Strikeout	An out made by a batter getting three strikes.
Strike Zone	In fast pitch, the space over home plate that is between the batter's armpits and the top of his knees. In slow pitch it is the space over home plate that is between the batter's back shoulder and his front knee.
Triple	A hit that allows the batter to reach third base.
Triple Play	Defensive play that results in three base runners being called out.
USOC	United States Olympic Committee. The governing body for all United States teams in Olympic Games.

Visiting Team   The team that journeys to another team's field for a game. The visiting team bats first at the "top" of an inning.

Walk   *See* Base on Balls.

11

Olympic and Softball Organizations

The organization of, and participation in, the Olympic Games requires the cooperation of a number of independent organizations.

The International Olympic Committee (IOC)

The IOC is responsible for determining where the Games will be held. It is also the obligation of its membership to uphold the principles of the Olympic Ideal and Philosophy beyond any personal, religious, national, or political interest. The IOC is responsible for sustaining the Olympic Movement.

The members of the IOC are individuals who act as the IOC's representatives in their respective countries, not as delegates of their countries within the IOC. The members meet once a year at the IOC Session. They retire at the end of the calendar year in which they turn 70 years old, unless they were elected before the opening of the 110th Session (December 11, 1999). In that case, they must retire at the age of eighty. Members elected before 1966 are members for life. The IOC chooses and elects its members from among such persons as its nominations committee considers qualified. There are currently 113 members and 19 honorary members.

The International Olympic Committee's address is—

Chateau de Vidy, CH-1007
Lausanne, Switzerland
Tel: (41-21) 621-6111   Fax: (41-21) 621-6216
www.olympics.org

The National Olympic Committees

Olympic Committees have been created, with the design and objectives of the IOC, to prepare national teams to participate in the Olympic Games. Among the tasks of these committees is to promote the Olympic Movement and its principles at the national level.

The national committees work closely with the IOC in all aspects related to the Games. They are also responsible for applying the rules concerning eligibility of athletes for the Games. Today there are more than 150 national committees throughout the world.

The U.S. Olympic Committee's address is—

Olympic House
One Olympic Plaza
Colorado Springs, CO 80909-5760
Tel: (719) 632-5551   Fax: (719) 578-6216
www.olympic-usa.org/

Softball Organizations

ASA/USA Softball
Director of National Teams
2801 N.E. 50th Street
Oklahoma City, OK 73111-7203
Tel: (405) 424-5266 Fax: (405) 424-3855
www.softball.org

International Governing Body
Federation Internationale de Softball (ISF)
1900 S. Park Road Plant City, FL 33566-8113 USA
Tel: (813) 707-7204, Fax: (813) 707-7209
E-mail: isfsoftball@ci.plant-city.fl.us
www.softball.worldsport.com

National Fastpitch Coaches Association (NFCA)
409 Vandiver Drive, Suite 5-202
Columbia, MO 65202
Tel: (573) 875-3033 Fax: (573) 875-2924
www.nfca.org

12

2000
Olympic Games

Team USA went to Sydney for the Olympic Games hoping to repeat its gold medal victory of 1996 and riding a winning streak of 110 games that began in 1998. The defending champions captured their second Olympic gold medal in September 2000, but to do it they had to bounce back from three consecutive extra-inning losses and stage one of the great comebacks in the history of the Games.

Japan, which lost to Team USA in the final, won the silver medal, and Australia took the bronze.

Round-robin Preliminaries

Team USA began round-robin play at Sydney with an outstanding game by pitcher Lori Harrigan, who threw a no-hitter for a 6-0 win against Canada. Harrigan allowed one runner to reach first base when she fumbled a ground ball in the first inning, then retired the next 20 batters. Team USA's six runs came on 10 hits, including home runs by shortstop Crystl Bustos, Dot Richardson (second base), and Jennifer Brundage (third base). With this victory, the U.S. squad extended its record winning streak to 111—including 48 international games, 60 summer touring games, and 3 exhibitions.

The following day, Cuba lost 3-0 to the U.S. team, which scored its first two runs on back-to-back home runs by Crystl Bustos and Sheila Douty in the second inning. Bustos had a second homer in the fourth inning, which supported the fine pitching of Danielle Henderson (two hits and seven strikeouts) and Christa Williams, who struck out five of the last six batters she faced. Even with three fielding errors, the U.S. team extended its winning streak to 112 games.

Two Olympic records were set when Team USA met its next opponent, Japan. First, the 11-inning game lasted 3 hours and 50 minutes—the longest ever in Olympic competition. Second, Team USA stranded 20 runners. A third record also fell—the 112-game winning streak of the U.S. team—as Japan won 2-1. The Japanese team played mistake-free ball, while four fielding errors and a succession of missed offensive opportunities contributed to the U.S. loss.

In the next game, against China, the U.S. team suffered a 14-inning, 2-0 defeat. Pitcher Michele Smith's Olympic-record 21 strikeouts weren't enough to overcome the team's continuing problems at bat. The Americans had just three hits and left 11 on base; through two games, that added up to 31 players stranded. In this game, a U.S. record was tied—it had been 18 years since a U.S. National Championship squad had lost two games in a row.

In a third consecutive extra-inning contest—this one lasted 13 innings—hitting problems continued to plague the U.S. team, which lost to Australia by a 2-1 score. Lisa Fernandez struck out 25, breaking Michele Smith's one-day-old strikeout mark, but surrendered the game-winning home run in the bottom of the 13th to Australia's Peta Edebone.

Recovering from a three-game slump, the U.S. team beat New Zealand 2-0 in the regulation seven innings. Lori Harrigan and Christa Williams limited New Zealand to one hit and struck out eight. Jennifer Brundage led the team in hitting with a home run and a single, while Lisa Fernandez had her first hit of these Games.

Fernandez then led the U.S. team to a 6-0 victory over Italy, striking out six during the first two innings of play and later hitting a two-run homer. Christa Williams pitched the last five innings and struck out seven. Altogether, the team scored six runs on five hits, while committing no errors.

Medal Rounds

In a semifinal matchup, China proved, once again, to be a tenacious opponent for the U.S. team. In eight innings, China's pitcher Zhang Yanqing struck out eight and allowed just four hits while walking two. But sharp work behind the plate by catcher Stacey Nuveman led to pickoffs of runners on first base in the second and seventh innings. Michele Smith, starting pitcher for the U.S. team, struck out 10 and gave up five hits in eight innings. Christa Williams followed and held the Chinese team hitless while allowing one walk. A three-run home run in the 10th inning by catcher Stacey Nuveman sent the American softball team into the medal round against Australia.

This game was as close as expected, with Team USA winning 1-0. Two fielding errors by Australia in the fifth inning led to the game's lone run, scored by Stacey Nuveman on Dot Richardson's two-out base hit. Lisa Fernandez went the distance, allowing just one hit and striking out 13. The victory was special for Fernandez, who had lost a perfect-game bid to Australia in the 1996 Olympic Summer Games and had pitched the record-setting 25-strikeout loss to Australia earlier in these Games.

Australia took the bronze medal, while the U.S. went on to face Japan in the gold medal game.

Going for the Gold

Japan entered the final with an unbeaten record in round-robin play that included breaking Team USA's 112-game winning streak and sending the defending champions into their three-game losing spiral. It was expected that this game would be low-scoring, and it was. Lisa Fernandez, starting for the second time in two days, allowed three hits and struck out eight. The two Japanese pitchers—starter Mariko Masubuchi and reliever Juri Takayama—gave up one hit and struck out six.

Japan scored first in the fourth inning on a home run that just sailed over the glove of outfielder Laura Berg. The U.S. came back to tie in the fifth inning with the team's first hit of the game—Stacey Nuveman's line drive to right-center field that brought Michele Smith home from second.

After seven innings of regulation play and with a light rain falling, the teams were tied at 1-1. But two walks from Japanese relief pitcher Juri Takayama in the bottom of the eighth inning opened the door for Laura Berg's shot to left-center field that was dropped by left fielder Shiori Koseki. The error brought Dot Richardson home from second base and produced the winning run and the final score of 2-1.

2000 Olympic Games Box Scores

USA Softball 2, Japan 1

Sep 26, 2000

Japan	000 100 00 - 1 3 1	(8-1)
USA Softball	000 010 01 - 2 1 1	(7-3)

WP-FERNANDEZ(2-1)
LP-Takayama A-8923
HR JAPAN - Utsugi

USA Softball wins the Olympic gold medal. A dropped ball in left allows Jennifer McFalls to score from 2nd in the 8th.

USA Softball 1, Australia 0

Sep 25, 2000

Australia	000 000 0 - 0 1 2	(6-3)
USA Softball	000 010 X - 1 5 0	(6-3)

WP-FERNANDEZ(1-1)
LP-Hardie T-1:33 A-8604

Lisa Fernandez throws a one-hitter with 13 strikeouts for Team USA. USA Softball advances to the gold medal game, where it will play Japan. Australia finishes the Olympic competition with the bronze medal.

USA Softball 3, China 0

Sep 25, 2000

China	000 000 000 0 - 0 5 0	(5-3)
USA Softball	000 000 000 3 - 3 4 1	(5-3)

WP-WILLIAMS(2-0)
LP-Yanqing T-2:45 A-8157
HR USAWOMEN - NUVEMAN (1)

U.S. wins its opening medal round game, advancing to bronze medal game. Stacey Nuveman hits a game-winning home run in the bottom of the 10th.

USA Softball 6, Italy 0

Sep 23, 2000

USA Softball	013 002 0 - 6 5 0	(4-3)
Italy	000 000 0 - 0 1 4	(2-5)

WP-WILLIAMS(1-0)
LP-Bugliarello T-1:53 A-7384
HR USAWOMEN - FERNANDEZ (1)

U.S. secures the final spot in the Olympic medal round. Lisa Fernandez and Christa Williams combine for a one-hitter.

USA Softball 2, New Zealand 0

Sep 22, 2000

USA Softball	010 100 0 -	2 6 1	(3-3)
New Zealand	000 000 0 -	0 1 1	(2-4)

WP-HARRIGAN(2-0) Save-WILLIAMS(2)
LP-Weber
HR USAWOMEN - BRUNDAGE (2)

Australia 2, USA Softball 1

Sep 21, 2000

USA Softball	000 000 000 000 1 -	1 5 0	(2-3)
Australia	000 000 000 000 2 -	2 2 0	(4-1)

WP-Harding
LP-FERNANDEZ(0-1)
HR AUSSIES - Edebone

U.S. pitcher Lisa Fernandez sets an Olympic record with 25 strikeouts. Australia's Peta Edebone hits game-winning home run in bottom of the 13th.

China 2, USA Softball 0

Sep 20, 2000

China	000 000 000 000 02 - 2 2 2	(3-1)
USA Softball	000 000 000 000 00 - 0 3 1	(2-2)

WP-Yanqing
LP-SMITH(0-2) T-3:57 A-3923

U.S. pitcher Michele Smith throws a two-hitter with 21 strikeouts. An error in the top of the 14th inning permits both runs for China.

Japan 2, USA Softball 1

Sep 19, 2000

Japan	000 000 000 02 - 2 7 0	(3-0)
USA Softball	000 000 000 01 - 1 11 4	(2-1)

WP-Takayama
LP-SMITH(0-1) A-3893

USA Softball's win streak is broken at 112 games. First win for Japan against the United States since the 1970 World event. U.S. leaves an Olympic-record 20 runners on base. Three errors in the top of the 11th inning result in both Japan runs.

USA Softball 3, Cuba 0

Sep 18, 2000

Cuba	000 000 0 - 0 2 1	(0-2)
USA Softball	020 100 X - 3 3 3	(2-0)

WP-HENDERSON(1-0) Save-WILLIAMS(1)
LP-Espinosa(0-1) T-1:32 A-3255
HR USAWOMEN - BUSTOS 2 (3), DOUTY (1)

Crystl Bustos hits two home runs for the U.S. Olympic Softball Team. The USA Softball Women's National Team has now won 112 consecutive games.

USA Softball 6, Canada 0

Sep 17, 2000

Canada	000 000 0 - 0 0 4	(0-1)
USA Softball	102 021 X - 6 10 1	(1-0)

WP-HARRIGAN(1-0)
LP-Bastarache(0-1) T-1:51 A-5210
HR USAWOMEN - RICHARDSON (1), BUSTOS (1), BRUNDAGE (1)

Lori Harrigan throws the Olympic's first individual pitcher no-hitter.

2000 Olympic Games
Overall Statistics for USA Softball

Sorted by batting average:

Player	AVG	GP-GS	AB	R	H	2B	3B	HR	RBI
Jennifer BRUNDAGE	.281	10-10	32	4	9	1	0	2	3
Crystl BUSTOS	.270	10-10	37	5	10	1	0	3	4
Leah O'BRIEN-AMICO	.226	10-10	31	0	7	0	0	0	2
Dot RICHARDSON	.179	9-8	28	1	5	0	0	1	3
Stacey NUVEMAN	.179	9-8	28	1	5	0	0	1	4
Laura BERG	.158	10-10	38	2	6	0	0	0	0
Sheila DOUTY	.156	10-10	32	4	5	1	0	1	3
Lisa FERNANDEZ	.097	9-9	31	3	3	0	0	1	2
Michele SMITH	.095	7-7	21	3	2	1	0	0	0
Christie AMBROSI	.063	9-8	16	0	1	0	0	0	1
Jennifer McFALLS	.000	8-2	7	2	0	0	0	0	0
Michelle VENTURELLA	.000	3-2	5	0	0	0	0	0	0
Christa WILLIAMS	.000	3-0	4	0	0	0	0	0	0
Totals	.171	10-10	310	25	53	4	0	9	22
Opponents	.082	10-10	291	7	24	2	0	2	3

LOB - Team (79), Opp (43). DPs turned - Team (4), Opp (6).

Sorted by earned run average:

Player	ERA	W-L	IP	H	R	ER	BB
Michele SMITH	0.00	0-2	27.2	9	4	0	5
Christa WILLIAMS	0.00	2-0	16.0	5	0	0	3
Lori HARRIGAN	0.00	2-0	12.1	1	0	0	1
Danielle HENDERSON	0.00	1-0	5.0	2	0	0	1
Lisa FERNANDEZ	0.47	2-1	29.2	7	3	2	4
Totals	0.15	7-3	90.2	24	7	2	14
Opponents	1.21	3-7	86.2	53	25	15	28